LEAN GOVERNMENT NOW!

INCREASE SERVICE, CAPACITY AND EMPLOYEE ENGAGEMENT WHILE REDUCING COSTS AND WASTES.

A STEP-BY-STEP TRAINING AND IMPLEMENTATION GUIDE WITH NUMEROUS LEAN GOVERNMENT EXAMPLES

HARRY W. KENWORTHY

Copyright © 2017 Quality and Productivity Improvement Center (QPIC, LLC) Press
Lean Government Center^{TM} Founded in 2008
Marlborough, Connecticut
All rights reserved.

www.leangovcenter.com

ISBN-13:978-1974223435
ISBN-10:1974223434

Forward and Acknowledgements

My Lean Government journey started providing pro bono consulting to the City of Hartford, Conn., in early 2005, applying Lean Six Sigma principles to help the City solve some of its pressing issues, most notably financial. The relationship with Hartford lasted for more than two years. This was a renaissance period for me, as I was able to see the how Lean Six Sigma, and more specifically Lean techniques, could be applied to the Government sector. I also learned that if you are providing services for free (pro bono), the less likely it is that the provided guidance, training, etc., will be taken seriously and successfully driven by your client. COO Lee Erdmann was the guiding force for Lean in Hartford. During the same period we also worked with private sector manufacturing clients implementing Lean Six Sigma and Lean.

The financial meltdown (the "Great Recession") that encompassed the country in 2008 -09 changed the landscape for virtually everyone. After losses to retirement/pension plans, real estate values, etc., Local, State and Federal Governments have suffered the most and many have not recovered to pre-recession status. Local and State Governments have been more impacted due to balanced budget requirements. Tax revenues from individual incomes, sales taxes, property taxes (declining land values), and casino revenues (many states have resorted to gambling as a revenue source) have all gone down significantly. At the same time, pensions, healthcare, Medicaid, Medicare, and Social Security costs have all continued to escalate. The monies to support pensions historically have relied on investing in stocks, bonds, hedge funds, dividends, etc. Government pension funds have continued to be overly optimistic about assumed return rates on investments.

In essence, the convergence of all of these factors has created the *perfect storm*, putting enormous pressures on Government to rein in spending and cut costs, or try to raise revenues (the *easy way out*). Unfortunately, Government services and capacity have been impacted in a negative way, including several cities going into bankruptcy – Detroit, MI, Central Falls, RI and Stockton, CA, as examples. Several states are in serious financial difficulty. Even though the economy is making a slow, painstaking recovery, unfortunately it appears that Government will have a difficult time following suit. We have clearly entered an age of *the new normal*. School systems are being hammered in many areas, with a reduction in teacher numbers that will increase classroom size and result in a reduction in the quality of education. As of the writing of this book, the United States Federal Government debt continues to increase at an alarming, unsustainable rate without resolution in Congress in sight.

This book is not intended to address the mandated programs and entitlements (the aforementioned pensions, healthcare, Medicaid, Medicare, and Social Security) that are in place. These will require hard work, legislation and political will (which many times is unwilling to change). Lean principles address the rest of the costs/wastes that are part of Government. Lean is the main vehicle to truly deliver *more with less*. Our experiences have shown that it's not unusual to find wastes of the magnitude of 50%+ in Government that can be reduced.

Active Lean initiatives, some with Six Sigma elements, are the favored approach in Government. They are in use or well underway, many based on state legislation, in the following states: Arizona, California, Colorado, Connecticut, Iowa, Maine, Michigan, Minnesota, Nebraska, New York, Ohio, Rhode Island, Tennessee, Washington, and Wisconsin. Initiatives are being also being set in motion in other states. So, momentum is building. Links to many of these websites (including some cities, counties and federal agencies) can be found at our Lean Government resource center: **http://leangovcenter.com/govweb.htm**. It's interesting to note that the statewide, city, county and K-12 Lean Government initiatives have been driven by both Democrat and Republican political leaderships. This reflects insightful leaders who *get it* when it comes to Lean. It's truly bi-partisan.

My first contact with Dr. W. Edwards Deming was in 1979, when I was part of a group of several hundred supplier executives invited to Nashua Corporation by Nashua's CEO, Bill Conway. Nashua sponsored a four-day seminar with Dr. Deming covering his 14 points for management. Dr. Deming was adamant that management owned the system and was responsible for a least 94% of the problems and management's job was to work on the system, with all of its related processes, to make things better for their employees. The employees, on the other hand, worked in the system and generally wanted to do a good job, with rare exception. I met Dr. Myron Tribus, who was formerly VP of Research & Development at Xerox and was later the Director of the Center of Advanced Engineering Studies (CAES) at Massachusetts Institute of Technology (MIT). Dr. Tribus was a close associate and advocate of Dr. Deming's principles and he organized a series of two-day seminars from 1983-85; on the first day Dr. Deming covered a condensed version of his 14 points and the second day was a series of industry practitioners who had applied some of those 14 points. I was selected to participate in seven of these second day sessions and learned from Dr. Deming when we had time at breakfast, lunch, and dinners. Dr. Deming introduced me to Jungi Noguchi, the director of the Japanese Union of Scientists and Engineers (JUSE). JUSE administered the prestigious Deming Prize in Japan and Mr. Noguchi arranged for me to tour several Deming Prize-winning companies, such as Hokushin and Fuji Xerox, during my numerous trips to Japan.

Spending nine years on the board of directors of a Japanese JV company, based in Nagoya, Japan (INOAC, MTP, a key tier one supplier to Toyota) was invaluable. I had the experience of seeing and understanding the Toyota Production System (TPS) first hand.

We adopted Dr. Joseph M. Juran's project-by-project approach in the mid-1980s and spoke at several Juran IMPRO conferences, along with meeting Dr. Blanton Godfrey (AT&T Labs and then later the CEO of the Juran Institute) and Joseph DeFeo (of Perkin Elmer and now CEO of the Juran Institute).

Dorian Shainin, who was well known for his excellent problem-solving techniques, always believed that *the parts were smarter than the engineers*. This meant going to the actual process work area to derive data from the process to identify the real problems. Applying Dorian's approach to Government would be *the process is always smarter that the managers*. He was an early advocate to *go to the Gemba* (work area) to truly see what is happening, which is integral in rapid improvement events (Kaizen events). Shainin believed that brainstorming, fishbone diagrams, and affinity diagrams were *organized guesswork* and, in my experience, he was right.

The Lean Enterprise Institute (LEI) formed in Cambridge, MA, via the MIT research work that James Womack and Dan Jones had done (**The Machine that Changed the World**) has become the most visible Lean organization along with the Shingo Institute (Shingo.org) at Utah State University.

My exposure to Lean was also influenced by my exposure to Jacobs Brake (a division of Danaher Corporation) in Bloomfield, CT, when George Koenigsaecker began his Lean journey in the 1980s, as I did some networking exchanges with George.

I'd also like to thank Harry Birkenruth, CEO of Rogers Corporation and my boss for many years. Harry is a true people person and a wonderful listener with great empathy for employees. He truly earned trust and respect among the employees in Rogers. He helped me form the model for what makes leaders successful (humility with high will) and this has been totally transferable to the Government environment.

As Vice President, Manufacturing for Rogers, I developed the worldwide Lean Six Sigma (LSS) initiative for the company. I was able to develop our training materials, in concert with GE (our selected Lean Six Sigma service provider), and then deploy this training in the US, Europe and Asia.

Dr. Jeffrey Liker, author of numerous books about the Toyota Production System and the Toyota Way, has also been an influence through my association with Dr. Liker and the Lean Leadership Institute.

Alan Robinson and Dean Schroeder have influenced me through personal discussion about ideas and daily Kaizen through their books *Ideas are Free* and *The Idea Driven Organization*. They also identified and re-invigorated Training Within Industry (TWI) that was developed during World War II to bring many US residents into the manufacturing workforce to support our war efforts. TWI has proven to be an effective means to supporting a key Lean approach - Standard Work (which will be discussed later in this book).

The Quality and Productivity Improvement Center (QPIC, LLC) began in 2004 providing Lean Six Sigma training, facilitating, consulting and coaching to clients. Government became our focus, forming the Lean Government Center in 2008 as a resource site for Lean Government initiatives.

Contributions for this book have come from Jeff Liker, Mary Jo Caldwell, Mark Graban, Alan Robinson, Dean Schroeder, Paul Akers, and Frank Gillern.

A special thanks to Cheryl Fenske who provided editing and her critical inputs which were invaluable.

Lastly, and most importantly, I would like to thank my wife and best friend Elaine, who has endured my work and travels over many years. Her inspiration, guidance and inputs have been critical in writing this book. Her extensive experience in education has also allowed QPIC to focus on Lean in K-12 education with great success.

Our daughters Rebekah and Amanda have also inspired me through their love and support.

Throughout this book, many clients will be held in confidence as we review what it takes to implement a successful, sustainable, Lean initiative in Government. We made sure, to the best of our ability, to use all materials with permission honoring any copyrights. If we have missed something, we apologize.

In summary, we do know that Lean Government is the best, most cost-effective and focused initiative/approach that serves the true customer, the taxpayer.

Table of Contents

Chapter 1
Brief History of Lean

Much has been written about the evolution and history of Lean. Lean started in the manufacturing sector and, some argue, from the time of Henry Ford and the Rouge Works Ford facility in Michigan making Model A cars and even before Ford. The modern day evolution has been really synonymous with Toyota and the Toyota Production System (TPS).

There have been many books written about Lean in great detail covering many of the concepts, tools and techniques referenced in this book. Searching through Amazon.com recently, there were 1,357 books or paperbacks on Lean manufacturing, 1,317 on Lean Six Sigma and 412 on Lean thinking. At any point in time, these numbers change. The intent of this book is not to go through a thorough historical exploration but rather to touch on the highlights and leave it to the reader's desire to search for more in-depth understanding through what is already available in the literature. To provide a brief historical perspective on the evolution of Lean, it's important to look at the contributions of: Frederick Taylor, Dr. W. Edwards Deming, Dr. Joseph M. Juran, Taiichi Ohno, Norman Bodek, Dr. Robert W. Hall, Dr. Richard J. Schonberger, Dr. James Womack and Daniel Jones, Dr. Jeffrey Liker, and Mike Rother.

Frederick Taylor

Taylor was the father of scientific management (the human component of production) in the early 1900s. He was focused on productivity improvements and inspecting quality before the product left the factory to try to ensure the quality was good and met the customers' needs.

Taylor's scientific management consisted of four principles:

1. Replace rule-of-thumb work methods with methods based on a scientific study of the tasks.

2. Scientifically select, train and develop each employee rather than passively leaving them to train themselves.

3. Provide detailed instructions and supervision of each worker in the performance of that worker's job.

4. Divide work nearly equally between managers and workers, so that the managers apply scientific management principles to planning the work and the workers actually perform the tasks.

Taylor's methods were used to render work repeatable, precise yet monotonous, leading to skill-reducing the tasks ("leave your brain at the door").

Dr. W. Edwards Deming

Dr. Deming was sent by the US Government, starting in 1947, to help Japan recover after being devastated in World War II. Dr. Deming presented a series of lectures that were well attended by Japanese top management who were intent on rebuilding their country, along with Japan's manufacturing base.

Dr. Deming's impact was well known inside and outside of Japan. Deming's 14 Points for Management[1] were developed as he conveyed his lessons to Japanese top management and refined by Dr. Deming over the years:

1. *Create constancy of purpose.*   Improve products and services to stay in business and provide jobs. Know what customers want and value.

2. *Adopt the new philosophy.*   Western management must awaken to the challenge, must learn their responsibilities, and take on leadership for change.

3. *Cease dependence on inspection to achieve quality.*   Build quality into the product or service to begin with. Inspection is normally seen as non-value added in Lean – extra steps that cost money to try to minimize rework or defects. Later in this book, the concepts of mistake proofing (poka-yoke), visual controls, process owners, standard work, root cause analysis, etc., will be covered.

4. *End the practice of awarding business on the basis of price tag.*   Instead, minimize total cost. Develop long-term supplier or service provider relationships. In the area of Government, the RFQ (Request for Quote), RFP (Request for Proposal), and other approaches are utilized to "get the best deal," along with competitive bidding to minimize the chance of favoritism. In reality, many of these RFPs and RFQs are written with not a good understanding of what Lean is, how it should be implemented, the cultural and leadership implications, and other factors. This leads to low bidders winning, which may have no correlation to the effectiveness of the implementation, or, in some cases, RFPs and RFQs are written with a specific service provider in mind, thereby getting around a competitive bidding process and creating a sham.

5. *Improve constantly and forever the systems of production and service to improve quality and productivity, and thus constantly decrease costs.* Total Quality Management (TQM) and Total Quality Control (TQC) became more prevalent over many years. This point could also be Kaizen – where:

   Kai = change and Zen = for the better leading to Kaizen = Continual Improvement[2]

6. *Institute training of the job*. The concept of Standard Work and Visual Controls utilizing Training Within Industry (TWI) approaches became the core means to ensure the training is accurate, effective, sustained and consistently in place.

7. *Institute leadership*. The aim of supervision should be to help people and machines do a better job. This reinforces the core of Lean leadership:
   - Have a very high respect for people in everything you say, do, and how you behave (leaders, managers, and supervisors).
   - The leader/manager's job is to provide the necessary coaching and training for your value added employees to identify and solve problems.

8. *Drive out fear.* That way everyone may work effectively for their organization. If there is excellent Lean leadership (point #7) in place, with a high respect for people, and they have conveyed a clear understanding that people will not lose their jobs as improvements are made and that's repeatedly communicated (supported by action and behaviors), then fear will be minimized. By implementing Lean, Government service and capacity will increase while wastes and costs will decrease. Attrition – not layoffs -- is the main means to deal with downsizing. Everyone, with very rare exception, wants to do a good job. It's the system created by management that causes frustrations, wastes, indifference and excess costs.

9. *Break down barriers between departments.* In Government there needs to be enhanced communications and coordination within and between departments and agencies. The "bigger picture" must be driven to the forefront and overcome political hurdles and operational silos.

10. *Eliminate slogans, exhortations and targets for the work force asking for zero defects and new levels of productivity*. Deming cited that the system was 94%+ controlled by management and members of the work force are victims of the system. This also enters into employee morale, which is driven by frustration for things being beyond the employee's control coupled with inconsistencies in supervision.

11. *Eliminate work standards (quotas) and management by objective (numbers). Substitute leadership.* This is known as "fashioning the club by which to be beaten with". Having standard work is different in that it sets the baseline and expectations for the current process so it runs smoothly and consistently. It also identifies where further wastes, errors and rework may happen, which provide more improvement opportunities which, in turn, get incorporated into the new level of standard work.

12. *Remove barriers that rob the worker of her/his right to pride of workmanship.* This goes back to point #7 Leadership, as supervisors are there to help all of their employees to

identify and remove wastes and identify and solve problems, leading to greater job satisfaction.

13. *Institute a vigorous program of education and self-improvement.* This is a basic tenet of Lean   to provide the necessary training and tools for employees to better service their customers (external and internal) by creating more value added services, while eliminating wastes. All employees should learn to become problem solvers.

14. ***Put everybody in the organization to work to accomplish the transformation.*** This means that Lean must be embedded in the culture of the organization so the work of Kaizen (daily or rapid improvement events) is in the forefront of what everyone is doing at all levels of the organization.

Deming, said (on page 315 of "Out of the Crisis"):

> *"I should estimate that in my experience most troubles and most possibilities for improvement add up to proportions something like this:*
>
> *94% belong to the system (responsibility of management)*
> *6% special"* [1]

Deming advocated that all managers need to have what he called a System of Profound Knowledge, consisting of four parts:

1. *Appreciation of a system:* understanding the overall processes involving suppliers, producers, and customers (or recipients) of goods and services;

2. *Knowledge of variation:* the range and causes of variation in quality, and use of statistical sampling in measurements;

3. *Theory of knowledge:* concepts explaining knowledge and the limits of what can be known; and

4. *Knowledge of psychology:* concepts of human nature.

Dr. Joseph Juran

Dr. Juran was also deployed to help Japan recover from World War II and was also very influential in shaping the approach that Japanese manufacturers would use to improve quality and evolve to continuous improvement. Juran considered defects to be "Operator-Controllable" if workers had working arrangements allowing them to meet quality standards. This means workers must have:

- **A means of knowing what is expected of them**
- **A means of knowing what is their actual performance**
- **The means for regulating their output, to reach conformance**

Juran concluded that management's job was unsuccessful if these three conditions were not met and the resulting defects were "management-controllable". These conditions are also embedded in what evolved as Standard Work within Lean. Juran's research (and that of others) shows the split of quality defects are (using the Pareto principle - 80% of the problems are caused by less than 20% of the potential sources):

- Management controllable - over 80%
- Operator controllable - under 20%

So, Deming and Juran both identified that the system which is developed and controlled by management plays the dominant role in the outcomes of the organization. As Deming has said, "Management works on the system, while the people work in the system" (paraphrased).

Juran's 10 steps for quality improvement[2] are:

1. **Build awareness of opportunities to improve**

2. **Set goals**

3. **Organize to reach goals**

4. **Provide training**

5. **Carry out projects to solve problems**

6. **Report progress**

7. **Give recognition**

8. **Communicate results**

9. **Keep score**

10. **Maintain momentum by making annual improvement part of the systems and processes of the company.**

Taiichi Ohno

Ohno was considered the father of the Toyota Production System (TPS)[3]. He was also the person who was given credit for developing the concept of the Seven Wastes (MUDA is waste in

Japanese), which are covered later in this book. Ohno also worked with Shigeo Shingo in Japan and was "discovered" by Norman Bodek of Productivity Press, who worked to translate Ohno's and Shingo's writings into English.

Masaaki Imai

Imai published his work in 1986 and popularized Kaizen[4], or continuous improvement, by describing in detail what Kaizen was and how it was being applied in Japan.

Norman Bodek

From a Western perspective, Bodek is credited with the identification of the revolution that was going on in Japan regarding quality and Lean, and more specifically related to Toyota through his leadership at Productivity Press.

Dr. Richard Schonberger

Dr. Schonberger held a series of seminars in the mid-1980s based on his work understanding what was happening in Japanese manufacturing and how it was being adapted in the United States. These workshop notes were incorporated into his book: *World Class Manufacturing*[5].

Dr. Robert Hall

Dr. Hall's book *Attaining Manufacturing Excellence*[6] was published in 1987 and covered the philosophy of Value Added Manufacturing in Chapter 2.

Dr. James Womack, Daniel Jones, and Daniel Roos

The Machine That Changed the World[7] is a book based on the Massachusetts Institute of Technology's $5 million, five-year study on the future of the automobile, written by James P. Womack, Daniel T. Jones (scientist), and Daniel Roos. This book did the most to foster the concept of Lean in manufacturing. John Krafcik, at MIT, is credited with coining the term "Lean". The focus for Lean is:

- **Add value for your customer.**
- **Value Stream Mapping – "Learn to See"**
- **Create Flow – "one-stop-shopping" goal**

- **Pull from the customer – keep pace with the customer demand rate**
- **Aim for perfection – "Right the first time" – eliminate errors and rework**

Dr. Jeffrey Liker

The Toyota Way[8] was the first book published by Dr. Liker in 2004 based on his in-depth studies of how the Toyota and the Toyota Production System (TPS) started and evolved to being the leading Lean organization in the world. Dr. Liker subsequently has published additional books looking at Toyota and its Lean principles and practices in greater depth.

Community Quality Initiatives start in the 1980s

A series of Community Quality groups ensued in the 1980-90s based on Dr. Deming's guidance, including the Philadelphia Council of Excellence (PACE); Madison (WI) Quality Improvement Network (MAQIN); the World Center for Community Excellence (WCCE) in Erie, PA; the Connecticut Quality Council (CQC); and others. These were groups that included manufacturing, service, healthcare, service and Government members to learn cooperatively from each other and utilize the principles of Total Quality Management (TQM). Just-In-Time (JIT – deliver what is needed in the exact quantity at the exact time it's needed) was also popular in the same timeframe, but it was misunderstood and misapplied by the automotive industry.

Six Sigma evolved out of Dr. Deming and Dr. Juran's teachings and was made popular by Motorola in the late 1980s and later was expanded by General Electric and its CEO, Jack Welch. Lean evolved out of the earlier work by Dr. Hall and Dr. Schonberger covering what was happening in Japan, followed by the work of Bodek at Productivity Press and Womack and Jones in their book on Toyota, *The Machine that Changed the World*. Lean was combined, by many organizations in the late 1990s, with Six Sigma to be known as Lean Six Sigma (LSS).

The Malcolm Baldrige National Quality Award was launched in 1988 and was focused on the following seven categories for organizational excellence:

> 1. *Leadership*
> 2. *Strategic Planning*
> 3. *Customer Focus*
> 4. *Measurement, Analysis and Knowledge Management*
> 5. *Workforce Focus*
> 6. *Operations Focus*
> 7. *Results*

The evolution of Lean through economic sectors has proceeded as follows (there have been a few exceptions to this, but this represents the general evolution):

> *Manufacturing*
> *Service*
> *Healthcare*
> *Government*
> *Education*

CHAPTER SUMMARY ON THE HISTORY OF LEAN: Lean has been in existence in many forms for many years. The tools and techniques are relatively easy to understand. There are no simple answers to deal with today's Government budgetary problems; however, what we do know is that Lean Government, encompassing Lean principles and a Lean management system, is the best, most cost-effective and focused initiative/approach that serves the true customer, the taxpayer.

REFERENCES:

[1]Deming, Dr. W. Edwards (1986). *Quality, Productivity and Competitive Position;* and Dr. W. Edwards Deming (1986); *Out of the Crisis;* both published by the MIT Center for Advanced Engineering Study.
[2]Juran, Dr. Joseph (1981). *Juran on Quality Improvement- Video series and workbook:* Juran Institute Inc.
[3]Ohno, Taiichi (1988). *Toyota Production System: Beyond Large-Scale Production;* Productivity Press.
[4]Imai, Masaaki (1986). *Kaizen: The Key to Japan's Competitive Success;* New York: Random House.
[5]Schonberger, Richard (1986). *World Class Manufacturing, The Lessons of Simplicity Applied;* the Free Press (a division of Macmillan).
[6]Hall, Robert W. (1987). *Attaining Manufacturing Excellence;* Dow Jones-Irwin.
[7]Roos, Daniel, Ph.D.; Womack, James P., Ph.D.; Jones, Daniel T. (1991): *The Machine That Changed the World: The Story of Lean Production*, Harper Perennial.
[8]Liker, Dr. Jeffrey (2004). *The Toyota Way;* McGraw-Hill.

Chapter 2
Leadership

*You get what you expect, inspect and enforce – organizational discipline
is normally lacking*

Lean leadership in Government[1] is a discipline that takes time and effort to master just like any other discipline. It takes years of experience, training and coaching to become a good accountant, a good engineer, a good carpenter and a good leader. Organizations tend to underestimate what it takes to become a good leader. How often does the most senior engineer get promoted to lead the engineering department simply because he/she was a really good engineer? Being a really good engineer, however, does not necessarily mean the person has the skills to effectively lead others. Providing appropriate leadership and coaching skills training is essential to developing leaders in an organization.

LEADERSHIP IS THE KEY
(Hopefully from the top executive)

Leadership owns and drives the culture. *Culture is "the way we do things around here."*

In a strong Mayor Government, Mayors are elected due to a need for change, term limits, popularity, etc., and yet may have not had any experience running a $500 million+ business (Government) with several thousand employees. This is coupled with their lack of knowledge of the technical aspects of how the city really runs and how and what each department really does. So the job falls to the current employees running the city departments to educate the new Mayor, unless they get swept out with the political tide (which can be even worse if the new appointees also don't know much about their new jobs). Unless there is a huge mandate for change, the current staff will move the new Mayor in the direction of status quo. The Mayor needs the knowledge and support of the incumbent department heads, so she or he is often unlikely to rock the boat for fear of being set adrift.

As an example, when we met with a new Mayor and an experienced police chief in a large city, after the initial review of the current state, we suggested that there was the potential to remove a lot of waste from operations to put more police officers on the street (community policing model). This was also based on the fact that the city had gone through five police chiefs in the previous seven years. We reviewed the procedures, forms and policies of the officers on the beat and found numerous areas of overlap and redundancies, along with many activities previously obsoleted that were still being rigorously undertaken. No one had really taken the time to see what was truly being done. The most recent police chief had come up through the technical track – officer on nights, sergeant, lieutenant, captain, deputy chief and finally chief --   30 years of service in the same system with some knowledge of alternative approaches to policing, but not Lean techniques. When the chief didn't want to hear anything about Lean, especially from consultants who had no knowledge of true policing, the Mayor sided with the chief. This was not an isolated incident in the cities we have worked with and also many state agencies.

When it comes to the City Manager-Council form of Government, we see a different scenario. City Managers, in general, have gone through a professional development track that has provided experience in a variety of Government functions, along with an understanding of best practices. The Alliance for Innovation, based in Phoenix, AZ and aligned with the International City/County Management Association (ICMA), provides professional networking and development for City Managers and their staff. Their mission statement reads: "*The Alliance for Innovation works to transform local Government and advance community excellence through the discovery and application of leading ideas and practices. The membership base consists of City Managers and other professionals in the City Manager form of Government.*" Of course, there are also other organizations to help develop mayors, such as the United States Conference of Mayors and the National League of Cities. With budgetary pressures intensifying over the last 8-10 years, less money is being spent to educate and develop State Agency Commissioners, Mayors, City and County Managers, and other elected and appointed officials in leadership positions.

There are leaders who went to the best schools, have been told how smart they are and are not afraid of letting everyone else know that via their words and/or actions. Their opinions are extremely strong and, even in the face of data and facts to the contrary, many times won't waiver. This can result in intellectual jousting matches when it comes to discussing and deciding on new, innovative approaches. This leader can also be big on creating win-lose situations when it comes to negotiations or decisions. Managers that work in this leader's organization see the ego and arrogance and usually have a low level of respect for the person, coupled with lower morale. The leader's respect for associates and their capabilities can be low. These are the leaders who are not going to go with a strategy or direction with which they are not familiar. This can change for several reasons:

1. A pocket of the organization does good innovation, embraces a different approach or change, such as Lean, and creates some impressive results.
2. A crisis causes the leaders to open their eyes and consider new options.
3. A respected peer uses Lean, has impressive results and shares the information. This can result in a strategic shift.

An example of a bright leader's negative impact was when we tried to develop a relationship and understanding of the leverage Lean could have in a State Commissioner's Agency. He listened patiently and shuffled through some papers at the same time. At the conclusion of our introductory overview on Lean he quickly stated, "I already know all about Lean and I know it doesn't work in Government." The body language from his key direct reports in the meeting was eye rolling and other signals that told us "this is the way he leads and there's no use in trying to proceed moving forward."

LEAN GOVERNMENT LEADER

It would be a misnomer to think that when we have our first conversation, the leader knows all about Lean. What we do know is that there are a series of characteristics and/or competencies that set these leaders apart and are closely aligned with the ability to successfully introduce change in their organization, truly shift the culture and sustain the improvements.

They are Servant Leaders in that they see their role as helping everyone to identify and eliminate problems. There is virtually no evidence of ego or arrogance in their actions.

Jim Collins' book, ***Good to Great***[2] identified a level 5 leader who "***built enduring greatness through a paradoxical blend of personal humility and professional will***" (Figure 2.1). Collins' work is well aligned with leaders being humble (high humility) coupled with a high respect for people.

Figure 2.1

They are open to understanding new approaches and are looking for new ways to leverage their budgets to deliver greater services and capacity to their citizens at lower costs. They are committed, deeply involved and directly participate in the Lean education and efforts. These leaders also are avid learners. Lean can't be seen as a leadership drive by or flavor of the month. This means that leaders should be Lean trainers and problem-solving participants. They lead by example and walk the talk.

They must create an environment where identifying and solving problems and removing waste is <u>expected</u> throughout the organization. This means that employees have to see and sincerely believe that leadership is serious about addressing problems that surface. Employees must be given the necessary Lean tools to identify and solve problems. Supervisors and managers must be given the necessary people skills and tools to solicit and help problems emerge and be solved. As Dr. W. Edwards Deming said, "You either have to change management, or you have to change management." This means that the necessary actions and behaviors of supervisors, managers and leaders must adapt and change to the new culture of continuously making problems visible and help their employees solve them. If the respective supervisors, managers and leaders refuse or can't adapt and change to this new way of acting and behaving, they must be removed from their positions.

> An excellent example of this was when Toyota created a joint venture (JV) with General Motors (GM) to create New United Motor Manufacturing Inc. (NUMMI) to make cars in Fremont, California in a plant that was previously run by GM. As one of the associates commented:
>
> "I like coming to work each morning. Before, when GM ran this place, I dreaded coming to the plant. Management was always screaming and hollering. Now it's so different! I look forward to getting here and helping my team solve problems". (Summer 1985, UAW Solidarity newsletter article)
>
> This was the old GM Fremont facility, one of the worst GM plants with a workforce that was viewed as being very bad – high grievances, low productivity, low quality, high absenteeism, poor safety, wildcat strikes, etc. Under the Toyota Production System (TPS) the plant was able to go from the worst to the best in GM in virtually all of the aforementioned categories, with the same UAW workforce, by changing the overall system – actions, behaviors, structure, and sub-systems. The change in leaders, managers and supervisors was profound under the mentoring of Toyota and Professor Edgar Schein of MIT.[3]

They believe that change is a constant. These leaders know that the dynamic of change will continue to accelerate, especially in the "new world" economic and budgetary environment. If they don't embrace change, change will embrace them. It's not enough to say that we have to manage change well. This must be complemented with a specific set of tools and strategies that create a much better chance for the change to be successful and sustainable.

They "Learn to See." They know that they need to get where the action is and talk to the people doing the actual work to really understand the problems/issues and help associates solve these problems. They know this is work that can't be done in their office or in a conference room. They also know they can't operate with rose-colored glasses, deny reality, or accept non-fact-based inputs that other managers are telling them.

They show respect to everyone. They operate with the golden rule in mind: "do onto others as you would have them do onto you." The Lean leader knows that clear responsibility and accountability is assigned for every process and for every problem that needs to be solved. They believe that, with rare exception, everyone really wants to do a good job. They also know that morale issues are more driven by the system, which management controls. They constantly look for what is wrong, not who is wrong – a focus driven on improving processes. Fixing processes and problems are their mantra, not figuring out who to blame.

They must have high integrity and earn trust. If this is not in place, the impact is huge. How can there be a strong team or high morale when the manager has low integrity and trust among his or her associates? This is earned by it's not what you say, it's how you say it; it's not what you do, it's how you do it; and the timing involved. If employees are your most precious resources (and they should be), treat them that way.

Integrity and Trust is one of the key competencies listed in the book ***For Your Improvement*** by Michael M. Lombardo and Robert W. Eichinger[4].

Individuals who are viewed as unskilled in Integrity and Trust:
- May hedge or not take a stand
- May treat others differently or indifferently at times
- May not walk her/his talk and be seen as inconsistent
- May have trouble keeping confidences and talks out of school
- Makes promises he/she can't keep
- May lack follow-through and causes problems for others
- Blames others for her/his own mistakes
- Seen as just out for her/himself

Skilled individuals in Integrity and Trust:
- Are seen as a direct, truthful individual
- Can present the unvarnished truth in an appropriate and helpful manner
- Keeps confidences
- Admits mistakes (can be appropriately self-deprecating)
- Doesn't misrepresent her/himself for personal gain

The most important core leadership competencies that Lombardo and Eichinger cite are:
Planning
Creativity
Strategic Agility

Motivating Others
Dealing with Ambiguity
Innovation Management
Building Effective Teams
Managing Vision and Purpose

They have the political will to get things done. They have a high understanding of what is for the greater good and then they figure how to maneuver through the political waters. Resistance to change is a large factor in getting things done. Tools, such as the Elevator Speech and the Stakeholder Analysis, are extremely useful for navigating and communicating changes (see Chapter 3).

They truly care about their people. They sincerely care to understand their associates' needs, wants and desires along with knowing about their families and life outside of work. This can't be faked, as people see right through it. They mean what they say, say what they mean and consistently demonstrate this in their actions.

THE LINKS WITH THE PROFESSIONAL ICONS:

With our client base in State agencies, large cities and counties and large K-12 school systems throughout the US, leadership is still first and foremost the key to sustainable Lean success, just as it is in the private sector. The major difference in the public sector is the political process which can certainly cause more frequent leadership turnover than in the private sector. If there is a shift in which political party took office, then the shift in direction can be deadly to initiatives that have been underway with the previous administration.

A notable exception to this was in Washington State when Governor Chris Gregoire was in her last year of office (2012) and initiated Results Washington, which was Lean-based. That fall was the new election for Governor with both Jay Inslee (Democrat) and Rob McKenna (Republican) running as strong Lean advocates, so no change in course was imminent. This was an unusual situation.

The quality "icons" have influenced the evolution of Lean leadership over time. Dr. W. Edwards Deming, Dr. Joseph M. Juran, Dr. Stephen Covey, and Dorian Shainin have all impacted Lean Leadership (as described in Chapter 1).

Dr. W. Edwards Deming[5]. It's clear that Deming's 14 points are interwoven into the fundamentals of Lean thinking, especially focused on the cultural aspects and employee development.

Dr. Deming also was focused on scientific problem solving and popularized the Plan-Do-Study-Act (PDSA) cycle which was modified by Japanese leaders to Plan-Do-Check-Act (PDCA). PDCA is a key scientific problem-solving methodology with Lean organizations today.

To summarize Dr. Deming's points and the impact on Lean leadership:
1. Focus on the process, not the people.
2. Develop and educate people – the most important resource in any organization.
3. Treat people with high dignity and respect and eliminate fear.

Dr. Joseph M. Juran[6]. Among the key items Dr. Juran covered in his handbook are:
- Project-by-project thinking – the forerunner to Six Sigma project sequence methodology
- Most of the Lean and Six Sigma tools that we know today
- How to establish the governance structure for Lean and Six Sigma, including roles and responsibilities
- Many of the change management concepts that impact cultural success

Dorian Shainin. Shainin was a firm advocate of what he called "statistical engineering". He developed many of his problem-solving principles for manufacturing during his time at Hamilton Standard and as a consultant at Rath & Strong before starting his own consulting firm. Shainin's statistical engineering techniques are well guarded intellectual property. The best insights into Shainin's work are through the book *"World Class Quality"* by Keki and Adi Bhote[7] through their experience with Shainin at Motorola.

Shainin strongly believed that "the parts are always smarter than the engineers". In Government, this translates to "the process is always smarter that the managers". This drove his problem-solving thinking. He viewed brainstorming, affinity diagrams and fishbone diagrams as "organized guesswork". He advocated going to where the process is actually happening and "seeing".

Shainin was a firm believer in the "Gemba (where the work is done) walk" and "Learn to See," well before these terms were commonly used and became core principles in Lean. These principles are fully translatable to Government value streams and processes.

Dr. Stephen Covey. His popular book, *The Seven Habits of Highly Effective People*[8], also influenced the Lean development process. Covey's seven habits are (Lean interpretation):
1. **Be Proactive** – Take the initiative to help associates identify problems and solve them. Set challenge targets.
2. **Begin with the End in Mind** – Have a goal for the future state after understanding the current state. It's always the pursuit of excellence, without ever getting there -- continuous improvement.
3. **Put First Things First** – Prioritize and work on the opportunities that have the greatest leverage.

4. **Think Win-Win** – We are not playing a zero sum game. Help others develop to create joint success. Win-lose management has many negative repercussions.
5. **Seek First to Understand, then to Be Understood** - Go the Gemba (where the work is done), observe and listen, and reflect on your level of understanding. Ask open-ended questions to develop scientific thinking in all associates.
6. **Synergy** – Assess the situation to know what cultural and Lean approaches can be leveraged or combined to make progress. Create synergy also from the application of Covey's first five habits.
7. **Sharpen the Saw** – Take time to re-energize and keep a fresh mind. Be a continuous learner.

From Womack and Jones (*The Machine That Changed the World: The Story of Lean Production*** [9] (Figure 2.2)**

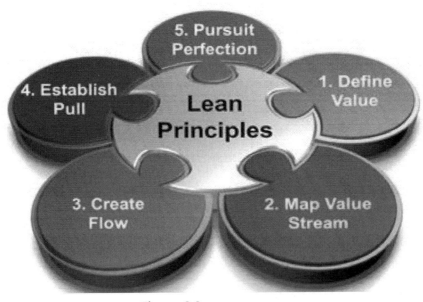

Figure 2.2

1. **Add value for your customer.**
2. **Value Stream Mapping – "Learn to See"**
3. **Create Flow – "one stop shopping" goal**
4. **Pull from the customer – keep pace with the customer demand rate**
5. **Aim for perfection – "Right the first time" – eliminate errors and rework**

Dr. Deming, Dr. Juran, Dorian Shainin, and Dr. Covey were all focused on improving processes and systems and they recognized that leadership must be focused on developing their people as this was the fundamental success driver.

From a Lean leadership approach, learning from Toyota and the published research by Dr. Jeffrey Liker[10,11] and Mike Rother[12] (Toyota Kata), we believe that *leaders can be made* through a desire to be continuous learners based on deliberate practice to develop their competencies and having a good coach mentoring them.

Leadership development does not happen by sitting in a classroom. We believe the model that works best is as follows (Figure 2.3):

1. Provide Lean leadership training and expectations in a classroom workshop setting. Make sure that everyone in the organization understands that everyone has a role in helping the organization shift to a Lean culture and help their leaders develop.
2. Conduct a leadership survey with several leaders first as a pilot. This should not be given to the entire leadership team.
   - The survey is done with inputs from direct reports (primarily); however, some peers and others should participate.
   - Survey information is compiled and summarized by an impartial source and given back to the leader to review and use to develop specific action plans.
   - The leader's action plans are then reviewed with an impartial source as a "reality check" and the plan is finalized by the leader.
   - The feedback and development plan is then shared by the leader with all of her/his direct reports and posted in the work area.
   - Face-to-face coaching and feedback are provided to the leader once the plan is established on a frequency that is most helpful (monthly at a minimum).
   - The survey is done again six months later as a follow up and results are reviewed again with the leader with progress discussed.
   - The core areas for Lean leadership are:
     o All leaders must transition from "telling" to "coaching"
     o All employees must develop proficiency in identifying and removing wastes and becoming problem solvers through leadership coaching
     o Employee huddles and a visual workplace must be in place
     o Learning and being coached about the required new skills (Figure 2.3) and turn new behaviors into ingrained, sustainable leadership habits

Figure 2.3

POLITICAL WILL - *Political will generally ain't willing*

In the Government sector, political will is a bigger challenge than the private sector. It's very unclear about the ability of elected officials to do what is for the "greater good". Robert Gates summed this up well:

Former Secretary of Defense Robert Gates said, "What has intrigued me is that the Congress lives in parallel universes. There is the fiscal restraint responsibility universe, which in general terms everybody signs up to, and then there's the specific universe, what's going to get cut in my state or district. And they're all against that. But if you can't close bases, if you can't end anything in any state, then where are you actually going to cut the defense budget?"

The elected official or appointee must be more sensitive to what is being done, why it is being done and what's in it for the affected stakeholders. In the context of stakeholders, Government sector leadership must be willing to deal with:

- Political party affiliation – Do you run the risk of crossing party lines, bipartisanship, going against the constituencies that allowed you to get elected, etc.?
- Public reaction and perception – We have all seen numerous examples of elected officials reacting to a lobbyist, union, trade organization or very few of their constituents to put forth legislative proposals and or funding decisions that are to the detriment of the "greater good".
- The ability to be re-elected or reappointed – As we explore root cause issues, the most common issue for the lack of political will and/or making decisions for the greater good seem to be political job sustainability and not offending your political party.
- The media – Public sector issues and information are more rapidly picked up by the press. Many instances/issues could be minimized or avoided by communicating much better up front to "get ahead" of the issue and create the framework/context in the proper perspective.

A conversation with a US Congressman in his local office in 2012 about the crisis in the US Postal System (USPS) over eliminating Saturday services to save money reflected the inability to grasp the overall situation and the failing business model vs. Federal Express, United Parcel Service and the Internet. It was déjà vu to the Robert Gates quote – *We can't cut postal deliveries on Saturday, because when I had my law practice, I wanted to get Saturday mail*. Everyone knows and agrees something has to be done as long as it's not in "their" district.

Using Lean to analyze the Fire Department effectiveness and deployment in a sizable Northeast city, a current state analysis indicated that only 10 fire station sites were necessary instead on the current 12. Personnel deployment on each shift needed to be realigned and redeployed from 12 stations to 10 and there needed to be a greater emphasis on fire prevention, since the main emphasis was always on fire suppression – saving lives and buildings. The city common council all agreed that the changes were necessary, yet each council member stated what amounted to "I'm in favor *as long as I have a fire station in my district."* There was a similar conversation about spending more time in the various fire station sites working with their neighborhoods on proactive fire prevention approaches, especially since it was clear that unattended kitchen fires were the #1 cause of fires. A recommendation to the Fire Department that more efforts should be placed on prevention, without the need to add any personnel, was a political hot potato.

On the bright side, there are examples where elected officials have exhibited the necessary political will, with their future political careers subordinated to what must be done for the greater good. One of the most striking examples of an elected official with high political will was Rhode Island's State Treasurer Gina Raimondo (now Rhode Island's Governor). In the weekend interview in the Wall Street Journal on March 23, 2012:

The former venture capitalist is a Democrat, which means that she believes in Government as a force for good. But "a Government that doesn't work is in no one's interest," she says. "Budgets that don't balance, public programs that aren't funded, pension funds that are running out of money, schools that aren't funded - How does that help anyone? I don't really care if you're a Republican or Democrat or you want to fight about the size of Government. How about a Government that just works? Put your tax dollar in and get a return out the other end."

As an elected Democrat in a heavily Democratic state, she was easily elected. Previously, as treasurer, Ms. Raimondo needed to address the Rhode Island pension system mess and not continue to kick the can down the political road. There were more people drawing a pension in Rhode Island than putting money into the pension system. Ms. Raimondo didn't view raising taxes as an option as the consequences would not be good for a state already in financial difficulties. This was highlighted by the town of Central Falls, RI, which was already in bankruptcy based on raising taxes to fund escalating pensions and seeing residents leave. Ms. Raimondo's efforts were based on a huge, long, relentless public education campaign to all corners of Rhode Island, meeting as many constituencies as she could. In essence, it was all about *doing the math* and the math she faced with the pension system in Rhode Island when she took office clearly didn't work. She persevered and changes were made to ensure pension solvency.

Although there are numerous examples of the lack of political will which far outweigh the examples of officials having political will, the main purpose of this discussion was to highlight that political will in Local, State and Federal Government entities remains a huge issue and requires special leadership. The better the problem definition and problem solving process with data-based decision making, the better the resulting solutions.

CONSOLIDATION AND REGIONALIZATION: Another opportunity to close budget gaps is to consolidate service centers through an effort to regionalize. Some examples:

• Regionalize school districts. Connecticut's 151 town districts and 17 regional districts have an enormous amount of duplication of functions outside of the classroom. Just think about the amount of curriculum directors there are in 168 districts! The State of Maryland has 24 school districts with a 66% greater population than Connecticut. Regionalization removes tremendous amounts of duplication, fragmentation and overlap in the non-classroom functions.   Regionalization does clash with the need for local autonomy and control. There is no question that there is a clear need for change. An example: establish much larger regionalized school purchasing cooperatives to leverage procurement costs and efficiencies. In another example of duplicative waste, Illinois has 859 school districts (2014-15).

• Duplicated costs between city or town and school administrations could be consolidated. Why do we need finance, human resources, purchasing and many other back office departments duplicated in the city and the school district? This, of course, is a matter of political will. In meetings in which we've participated, school boards and city councils both agree this duplicated effort is wasteful, yet neither wants to give up their turf. The result is status quo. While there are some cities where some consolidation has taken place, it is, however, a small minority.

• The Phoenix 911 dispatch center is an excellent example of the value of consolidation. This center coordinates emergency response calls for 21 Phoenix valley cities. Eight of the cities in the Phoenix Valley (Phoenix included) have populations in excess of 150,000 residents. In other parts of the country, this would result in eight different 911 centers.

LEGISLATION, STATUTES, AND ORDINANCES

It seems generating any form of legislation is hampered by a lack of understanding of the real problem. When a group is drawn together to solve a problem, rarely is a consensus built to have everyone on board agree to the problem statement. This is easy to recognize in any meeting when someone presents a problem and the group immediately moves into solution mode. How do we know what is the right solution if we haven't a clear agreed upon problem statement?

Data-based legislation Figure 2.4) is an approach to address these issues:

Proposed Legislation Title:		Impact Location:	

Business Case for Legislation:

Legislation Problem Statement:

Legislation Scope:

IN

Legislation Goal:

Expected Direct Benefits: (savings)	
Expected Indirect Benefits: (savings)	
Expected Costs (independently verified): (costs)	

Out

Impacted Existing Legislation:			Impacted Constituents:		
Which?			Who?		
Modify?			Where?		
Obsolete?			How many?		

Timeline:	Initial	Target	Update					

Other:

Figure 2.4

Why use a charter document (Figure 2.4)? It forces the hard work to be done to reach consensus before proceeding with any proposed legislation. The elements of a Data Based Legislation Charter document are as follows:

1. Problem Statement – First and foremost, this requires the dominant amount of work to truly explore all elements of "what is the problem we're trying to address?" This is the hard work that must be done. Alignment is critical for all parties involved to listen and explore all avenues to properly vet the problem to be addressed in order to have all involved reach agreement before proceeding any further. It can take 70-80% of the time to develop and fill out the entire charter document. Facts and data must be explored here rather than relying on opinions and emotions and this prevails throughout the charter document.

2. Business Case for the Legislation – This block addresses the "so what" response to the Problem Statement. What is the financial impact of solving this problem? What is the citizen, regulatory, etc., impact of solving this problem? How does this fit with the overarching Government key goals? If there isn't a strategic fit or other factual compelling reason, why would we want to do this?

3. Legislation Scope – This defines the areas that will and won't be impacted by the legislation. Scope also addresses the need to drive to have a singular area, department, or agency be responsible to own and execute the legislative output. Cross-functional confusion, duplication and overlap must be eliminated.

4. Legislation Goal – This is a clear, concise statement of the goal of the legislation and how we plan to measure its level of effectiveness. There must be a mechanism to follow through and ensure the legislation that is being put in place is being measured regarding its intended consequences.

5. Expected Benefits – Time must be spent developing the expected direct and indirect benefits of implementing the proposed legislation. Direct benefits are more related to money, while indirect benefits are more focused on service and impact – speed, freed up time to focus on other areas, reducing error and rework rates, etc.

6. Expected Costs – This should not be glossed over. It's important to clearly understand all the associated costs in moving forward with the legislation. Clarifying the benefit-cost relationship is critical, especially in these more difficult economic times for Government.

7. Impacted Current Legislation – Is there overlap with the proposed legislation and already existing legislation? More Government entities are taking a more serious look at this area. Memories are sometimes short about what is already on the books.

8. Impacted Constituents – This section focuses on an in-depth review of all potential effected stakeholders, both internal to the Government and external (business impact, environment, energy, etc.).

Several states have been eliminating legislative wastes. Agencies are addressing the current legal mandates and determining which ones need to be rescinded, combined or rewritten. This has been especially beneficial with mandates related to the costs of establishing and doing business, which has positive economic benefits.

Another critical aspect of legal mandates is to examine if they are being followed as they were originally written and intended, or have they morphed over time into something else based on interpretation and the passing of verbal training instructions.

Before starting a process improvement effort, all of the legal mandates related to the process should be fully scrutinized regarding the facts versus the beliefs. Doing this can eliminate wasteful process steps that don't even need to be done (see Chapter 4 - Customers).

EVIDENCE-BASED POLICYMAKING

An article written by Quentin Palfrey[13] discussed 2016 legislation enacted creating a federal Commission on Evidence-Based Policymaking. Palfrey covered five concrete steps that can be taken to ensure a more prudent use of taxpayer money:

1. "Add requirements and support of rigorous evaluation into existing funding streams." The focus here is to run pilots of new services and compare them to existing services to determine statistical significance.
2. "When allocating scarce resources to oversubscribed programs, consider determining eligibility by lottery rather than first-come-first-served."
3. "Require that agencies link administrative datasets."
4. "Institutionalize best practices by creating independent evaluation offices." These offices make objective assessments with data/evidence to improve programs. Benchmarking can also be helpful here to learn best practices from others (more on Benchmarking in Chapter 5).
5. "Take a page from Congress' book by establishing state-level commissions on evidence-based policymaking."

COLORADO'S 'PITS AND PEEVES INITIATIVE'[14]

This was an initiative started by Colorado's Governor Hickenlooper in 2011 with an extensive series of Colorado stakeholder roundtables with participants from approximately 100 business and community organizations to identify "red tape". The outcome was The Governor's Executive Order 2012-002, fondly called "Pits and Peeves". The issues that were addressed regarding the need for change in Governmental culture:

- Regulatory inefficiencies and delays
- Need for greater coordination among agencies, such as information sharing and consistency of administrative approaches
- Need for better coordination between federal and local agencies to achieve regulatory coherence and avoid conflicting or inconsistent requirements
- Need for periodic review of agency rules and regulations to evaluate continued need and effectiveness
- Need to make better use of available technology to improve communication and interaction with the public
- Need for a go-to person in each agency to help customers navigate the agencies' systems
- Need to pay greater attention to economic and unintended adverse impacts of proposed regulations, requirements and procedures
- Need to pay more attention to ensuring that new regulations reflect legislative intent

Using Colorado's example, the case is clearly made for the need to do a complete review of all current legislation on the books to see if it can be eliminated, modified or combined. Unfortunately, these introspective looks are few and far between, often displaced by the "need" to generate more legislation.

CHAPTER SUMMARY ON LEADERSHIP: When we speak at conferences or meet with various groups, individuals lament that they would love to move forward with Lean, but their leader doesn't want to. Our answer is that anyone who has a team of employees can apply the Lean principles in this book. There is nothing holding you back, other than you! Implement the principles and make the changes. Your level of employee engagement and morale will dramatically go up. Your results will cause others – maybe even your organization's leader -- to notice.

The great recession has heightened the need for Government to utilize Lean to reduce wastes and costs (balance budgets) and improve capacity, service and employee engagement. Lean is truly a way to "do more with less" and create a better, faster, less expensive Government.

REFERENCES:

[1]Kenworthy, Harry (2016). *Lean Leadership in Government*; American Society for Quality, Government Division News; Spring 2106, Volume 19, No. 1, pages 13-18.
[2]Collins, Jim (2001). *Good to Great*; Harper Collins Publishers.
[3]Shook, John (Winter 2010). *How to change a culture: lessons from NUMMI;* MIT Sloan Management Review, Volume S1, No 2, pages 63-68
[4]Lominger, Michael and Eichinger, Robert (1996). *For Your Improvement*: Lominger Limited, Inc.
[5]Deming, Dr. W. Edwards (1986). *Out of the Crisis*; MIT-CAES.
[6]Juran, Dr. Joseph M. and Gryna, Frank (1988). *Juran's Quality Control Handbook, 4th Edition*; McGraw Hill.
[7]Bhote, Keki R. and Bhote, Adi K. (2000). *World Class Quality: Using Design of Experiments to Make it Happen, 2nd Edition*; AMACOM.
[8]Covey, Stephen R. (1989) *The Seven Habits of Highly Effective People*; Simon and Schuster.
[9]Roos, Daniel, Ph.D.; Womack, James P., Ph.D.; Jones, Daniel T. (1991): *The Machine That Changed the World: The Story of Lean Production.* Harper Perennial.
[10]Liker, Jeffrey and Trachilis, George (2015). *Developing Lean Leaders at all Levels: A Practical Guide:* http://www.amazon.com/Developing-Lean-Leaders-all-Levels/dp/0991493230/ref=sr_1_2?s=books&ie=UTF8&qid=1449258235&sr=1-2&keywords=jeff+liker
[11]Liker, Jeffrey and Convis, Gary (2011). *Toyota Way to Lean Leadership*: http://www.amazon.com/Toyota-Way-Lean-Leadership-Development/dp/0071780785/ref=sr_1_3?s=books&ie=UTF8&qid=1449258235&sr=1-3&keywords=jeff+liker
[12]Rother, Mike: *Toyota Kata*; http://amzn.to/1kJ0xF

[13]Palfrey, Quentin (2/27/2017). *5 Strategies for Evidence-Based Policymaking*; Governing

[14]https://sites.google.com/a/state.co.us/pits-and-peeves-dev2/home/the-process

REFERENCE MATERIALS FOR FURTHER READING:

Shook, John and Rother, Mike (1999). *Learning to See: Value Stream Mapping to Add Value and Eliminate MUDA.* Lean Enterprise Institute.

Chapter 3
Change Management

In the absence of clear, credible communications, the rumor mill will fill the void and it's never what you want.

One of Dr. W. Edwards Deming's quotes during his famous four day seminars to top management attendees was: "You either have to change management, or you have to change management". The implications were obvious: either get management on board or get them out of the way so they don't hamper/undermine forward progress. Introducing a change initiative, or just even a "minor" change, is a leadership challenge. It's not about the new idea; it's about the acceptance of the new idea into the culture and successfully sustaining it.

We define culture as "the way we do things around here". We view the components of culture as the actions, behaviors, systems and structures that are in place in the organization which creates and sustains "the way we do things around here". If the desire is to have a "Lean culture", then there needs to be a permanent shift in the actions, behaviors, systems and structures to support this new culture. Changing the culture is the hardest part organizations have to do in order to create a successful, sustainable Lean implementation. There must an intellectual leap from merely trying to use a set of Lean tools & techniques on a sporadic basis, to imbedding Lean into the culture and strategy of "how we do business around here" and ultimately creating a Lean Management System. Few leaders and their organizations successfully understand what is required, get impatient, and move on to other horizons. There certainly can be pockets of great Lean success within organizations at lower levels, based on the leaders in those respective areas.

It's about managing change (Figure 3.1)

The acceptance of change timeline:

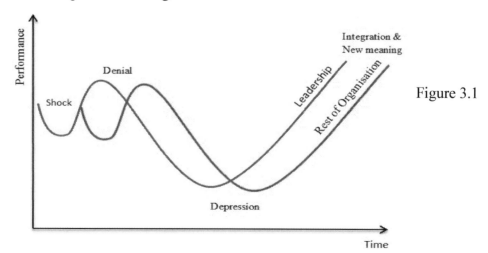

Figure 3.1

In Figure 3.1 we see the timeline phases that leadership and the rest of the organization experience when going through a change. We obviously want leadership to be in the lead. So the phases of change (there are many different models) are:

- Shock – There is something new going on that's a change from the status quo that scares us. We haven't experienced this before and we are surprised at this new direction the organization is going in. Why are we doing this?
- Denial – This won't really happen. We can't possibly be doing this. There is no reason for us to do this.
- Depression – This is the worst it's ever been here. When will this ever get over? I don't want to come to work.
- Integration & New Meaning – This is the acceptance phase. I now understand the value of doing this. I'm glad we are moving in this direction. This will make things better for everyone.

Dr. John Kotter's Approach to Change

There are certainly enough books written about successfully managing change. Dr. John Kotter, in particular, has been widely followed, starting with his book *Leading Change* [1], which is widely viewed as the "bible" for cultural change in organizations.

Dr. Kotter has proven over his years of research that following *The 8-Step Process for Leading Change* will help organizations succeed in an ever-changing world.

In Kotter's view (Figure 3.2), some general rules about cultural change include:
- Cultural change comes last, not first.
- You must be able to prove that the new way is superior to the old.
- The success must be visible and well communicated.
- You will lose some people in the process.
- You must reinforce new norms and values with recognition and rewards (monetary rewards aren't likely in Government) – promotions are possible.
- Reinforce the culture with every new employee.

Step 1:

Establishing a Sense of Urgency

- Examine market and competitive realities, and identify and discuss crises, potential crises, or major opportunities

Step 2:

Creating the Guiding Coalition

- Assemble a group with enough power to lead the change effort, and encourage the group to work as a team

Step 3:

Developing a Change Vision

- Create a vision to help direct the change effort, and develop strategies for achieving that vision

Step 4:

Communicating the Vision for Buy-in

- Use every vehicle possible to communicate the new vision and strategies, and teach new behaviors by the example of the Guiding Coalition

Step 5:

Empowering Broad-based Action

- Remove obstacles to change, change systems or structures that seriously undermine the vision, and encourage risk-taking and nontraditional ideas, activities, and actions

Step 6:

Generating Short-term Wins

- Plan for visible performance improvements, create those improvements, recognize and reward employees involved in the improvements

Step 7:

Never Letting Up

- Use increased credibility to change systems, structures, and policies that don't fit the vision, also hire, promote, and develop employees who can implement the vision, and finally reinvigorate the process with new projects, themes, and change agents

Step 8:

Incorporating Changes into the Culture

- Articulate the connections between the new behaviors and organizational success, and develop the means to ensure leadership development and succession

Figure 3.2

Here is a list and discussion of the 24 attacks, mentioned by Kotter[1], that have been used quite commonly. As you will see, they all draw on one or more strategies based on confusion, fear mongering, death-by-delay, or ridicule and character assassination. There are many more slight variations on these 24, but these two dozen seem to be the most basic and confounding. There is also a response to each of the attacks which will not silence valid criticism, but will help stop verbal bullets from killing good ideas.

#1 "We've been successful, why change?!"
Attack:
We've never done this in the past and things have always worked out OK.
Response:
True. But surely we have all seen that those who fail to adapt eventually become extinct.

#2 "The only problem is not enough money."
Attack:
Money is the issue, not _____ (computers, product safety, choice of choir songs, etc).
Response:
Extra money is rarely what builds truly great ventures or organizations.

#3 "You exaggerate the problem."
Attack:
You are exaggerating. This is a small issue for us if it is an issue at all.
Response:
To the good people who suffer because of this problem, it certainly doesn't look small.

#4 "You're saying we've failed??!!"
Attack:
If this is a problem, then what you are telling us is that we have been doing a lousy job. That's insulting!
Response:
No, we're suggesting that you are doing a remarkably good job without the needed tools (systems, methods, laws, etc) which, in our proposal, you will have.

#5 "What's the hidden agenda?"
Attack:
It's clear you have a hidden agenda and we would prefer that you take it elsewhere.
Response:
Not fair! Just look at the track record of the good folks behind this proposal! (And why would you even suggest such a thing?)

#6 "What about this, and that, and that (etc.)?"

Attack:

Your proposal leaves too many questions unanswered. What about this and that, and this and that, and...

Response:

All good ideas, if they are new, raise dozens of questions that cannot be answered with certainty.

#7 "No good! It doesn't go far enough" (or, "It goes too far")

Attack:

Your proposal doesn't go nearly far enough.

Response:

Maybe, but our idea will get us started moving in the right direction, and do so without further delay.

#8 "You have a chicken and egg problem."

Attack:

You can't do A without doing B, yet you can't do B without doing A. So the plan won't work.

Response:

Well actually, you can do a little bit of A which allows a little bit of B which allows more A which allows more of B, and so on.

#9 "Sounds like 'killing puppies' to me!"

Attack:

Your plan reminds me of a thing disgusting and terrible (insert totalitarianism, organized crime, insanity, or dry rot...)

Response:

Look, you know it isn't like that. A realistic comparison might be...

#10 "You're abandoning our values."

Attack:

You are abandoning our traditional values.

Response:

This plan is essential to uphold our traditional values.

#11 "It's too simplistic to work."

Attack:

Surely you don't think a few simple tricks will solve everything?

Response:

No – it's the combination of your good work and some new things that, together, can make a

#12 "No one else does this!"
Attack:
If this is such a great idea, why hasn't it been done already?
Response:
There really is a first time for everything and we do have a unique opportunity.

#13 "You can't have it both ways!"
Attack:
Your plan says X and Y, but they are incompatible. You can't have both!
Response:
Actually, we didn't say X or Y—although, I grant you, it may have sounded that way. We said A and B, which are not incompatible.

#14 "Aha! You can't deny this!"
Attack:
I'm sorry – you mean well, but look at this problem you've clearly missed! You can't deny the significance of this issue!
Response:
No one can deny the significance of the issue you have raised, and, yes, we haven't explored it. But every potential problem we have found so far has been readily solved. So in light of what has happened again and again and again, I am today confident that this new issue can also be handled, just like all the rest.

#15 "To generate all these questions and concerns, the idea has to be flawed."
Attack:
Look at how many different concerns there are! This can't be good!
Response:
Actually, many the questions mean we are engaged, and an engaged group both makes better decisions and implements them more successfully.

#16 "Tried it before – didn't work."
Attack:
We tried that before and it didn't work.
Response:
That was then. Conditions inevitably change [and what we propose probably isn't exactly what was tried before]

#17 "It's too difficult to understand."
Attack:
Too many of our people will never understand the idea and, inevitably, will not help us make it happen.
Response:
Not a problem. We will make the required effort to convince them. It's worth the effort to do so.

#18 "This is not the right time."
Attack:
Good idea, but it's the wrong time. We need to wait until this other thing is finished (or this other thing is started, or the situation changes in a certain special way).
Response:
The best time is almost always when you have people excited and committed to make something happen. And that's now.

#19 "It's too much work."
Attack:
This seems too hard! I'm not sure we are up for it.
Response:
Hard can be good. A genuinely good new idea, facing time consuming obstacles, can both raise our energy level and motivate us to eliminate wasted time.

#20 "Won't work here, we're different!"
Attack:
It won't work here because we are so different.
Response:
Yes it's true, we're different, but we are also very much the same.

#21 "It puts us on a slippery slope."
Attack:
You're on a slippery slope leading to a cliff. This small move today will lead to disaster tomorrow.
Response:
Good groups of people—all the time-- use common sense as a guard rail to keep them from sliding into disaster.

#22 "We can't afford this."
Attack:
The plan may be fine but we cannot do it without new sources of money.
Response:
Actually, most important changes are achieved without new sources of money.

#23 "You'll never convince enough people."
Attack:
It will be impossible to get unanimous agreement with this plan.
Response:
You are absolutely right. That's almost never possible, and that's OK.

#24 "We're not equipped to do this."
Attack:
We don't really have the skills or credentials to pull this off!
Response:
We have much of what we need and we can and will get the rest.

Another popular change management approach is the ADKAR model (Figure 3.3 from PROSCI[2]):

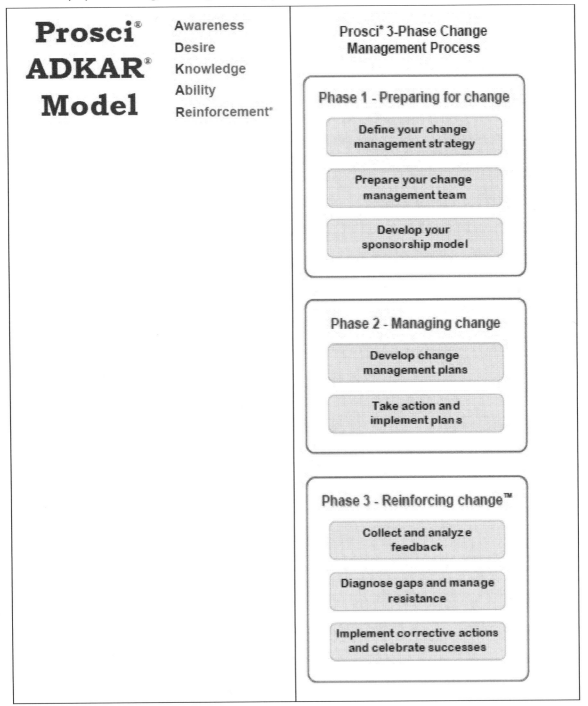

Figure 3.3

Of course, there are other change management models which can be Googled. The main takeaway is that the management of change is usually ignored, responded to too late, or not well planned for. This is critical work that must be planned for from the beginning of the Lean journey and consistently executed throughout the journey.

THE TOYOTA PRODUCTION SYSTEM (TPS) It's also important to understand why the culture of the Toyota Production System has been the most successful embodiment and synonymous with Lean excellence. In **_The Toyota Way_**[3], Jeffrey Liker talks about 14 principles of Toyota Production Systems (TPS). Although Toyota is a car manufacturer, these principles are universally adaptable to any organization, including Government:

1. Base your management decisions on a long-term philosophy, even at the expense of short-term financial goals.

2. Create a continuous process flow to bring problems to the surface.

3. Use "pull" systems to avoid overproducing.

4. Level out the workload (Work like the tortoise, not the hare.)

5. Build a culture of stopping to fix problems, to get quality right the first time.

6. Standardized tasks and processes are the foundation for continuous improvement and employee empowerment.

7. Use visual control so no problems are hidden.

8. Use only reliable, thoroughly tested technology that serves your people and processes.

9. Grow leaders who thoroughly understand the work, live the philosophy, and teach it to others.

10. Develop exceptional people and teams who follow your organization's philosophy.

11. Respect your extended network of service partners and suppliers by challenging them and helping them improve.

12. Go and see for yourself to thoroughly understand the situation ("learn to see" where the work is actually done).

13. Make decisions slowly by consensus, thoroughly considering all options; implement decisions rapidly.

14. Become a learning organization through relentless reflection and continuous improvement (kaizen).

These principles also create small to significant changes that need to be made in the leadership approach to an organization's culture, which ties back into Kotter's work.

It's not this book's intent to delve deeply into the works of Dr. Kotter, Prosci's ADKAR model or the culture of TPS as many books have already been written on these topics.

There are, however, two very effective tools that are universally useful in coping with the resistance to change, and also for enhanced communications: the Elevator Speech and the Stakeholder Analysis.

THE ELEVATOR SPEECH

It's called an elevator speech for the purpose of conveying the following key points in the span of about 90 seconds, or less (an elevator ride):
  1. What is the change?
  2. Why are we doing it?
  3. What do you expect from me?
  4. What's in it for me (WIIFM)?

- It's a tool for sharing a vision – it could be an organization-wide initiative, or it could be for a particular project.
- It's a means of explaining to all of the affected segments that are touched by the change or project what it's all about.
- It should be simple and easily understood.

The elevator speech should be used in a variety of settings:

1. A major change initiative launch – in this case, Lean Government. For example, St. Louis County, Missouri:
   What are we doing?
   We are the champions for continuous improvement across county Government.

   Why are we doing it?
   So that St. Louis County Government serves customers better, faster, and with greater impact.

   What do you expect out of me?
   Participation, collaboration and commitment – sharing your ideas and suggestions and staying the course until improvement results are realized!

   What's in it for me?
   An opportunity to do satisfying work that makes a difference every day.

2. Any projects that are undertaken. An example from an Accounts Payable Kaizen event in Des Moines, Iowa, Public Schools:

What are we doing?

Identify problem areas as they relate to the AP disbursement process,

- Inefficiencies
- Timeliness
- Accuracy

Why are we doing it?

Enhance the disbursement so we free up resources and be more mission-based

- To cut processing costs
- Uniform in our processes

What do you expect out of me?

- Open-mindedness
- Cooperation
- Share ideas
- Be an Advocate

What's in it for me?

- More time
- Less frustration
- Clearly defined roles and responsibilities

3. Any changes where resistance is anticipated. An example with a city's new timekeeping system:

What are we doing?

We're introducing a new timekeeping system and there will be training for everyone the week of February 10th.

Why are we doing it?

Our previous timekeeping system was put in place in the early 1980's and has many manual transactions related to it that has led to numerous errors and rework.

What do you expect out of me?

Take the necessary training and make sure to ask questions about any elements of the new system that are unclear. Give the new system a try and report any issues you find.

What's in it for me?

Accurate paychecks the first time creating less wasted time and personal frustrations resolving inaccurate pay issues.

An elevator speech is developed and owned by the involved parties. In the case of a major organization wide initiative, the leader and top management team would get together and first clearly understand what the change is and individually write their own elevator speech. The individual speeches would then be paired up, shared, and enhanced, with the ultimate outcome of a consensus speech being developed and owned by the team. Everyone has "skin in the game" in the development of the speech vs. a speech that's given to the group by the leader. In the case of projects, such as Kaizen events, the same development and ownership process would take place in developing the elevator speech for the project by the project team.

How often does it happen when people get assigned to work on projects without having a clear understanding of why they are there and what the project is all about? At times, this lack of clarity is communicated to others such as "I don't know why they told me to go to that meeting"; "I'm not sure what this project is supposed to do and/or is it worth doing?" and other similar comments. This gets the project off to a shaky start, along with others not involved with the project receiving a negative view, which could create further resistance to what is being done, even as the project just gets underway.

Another example of an elevator speech from a school district working on a Kaizen event to improve their grants process (Figure 3.4) (to be able to acquire more outside funding for the school district by eliminating non-value added steps and enhancing the value added aspects of the process):

What is the project?
>   We are working on designing and communicating a district-wide process for competitive grant applications.

Why are we doing it?
>   The district is losing opportunities and grant revenue due to redundancy/multiple applications to funders. The district lacks any meaningful statistics for reporting on success to stakeholders. Finally, without a clear, defined process the district cannot ensure equity in grant funding.

What do you expect out of me?
>   We expect you to participate in, provide feedback on, and support the grant application process.

What's in it for me?
>   As a result of a well-defined competitive grant application process there will be more resources (both funding and personnel), less surprises/scrambling to find information, and increased understanding of how/from whom to get help. We will also learn new Lean tools.

Figure 3.4

Elevator speeches are underutilized and can significantly enhance communications related to any changes and help get out in front of any resistance that could form.

THE STAKEHOLDER ANALYSIS

The Stakeholder Analysis is another critical tool that usually works in concert with the Elevator Speech to communicate changes and minimize resistance to change.

Therefore, it's necessary to identify those individuals or groups with an interest in the process or are impacted by the process and what their positions on a particular change initiative (Lean) might be. These are the stakeholders. The Stakeholder Analysis can be done at the organization, unit, group, project, etc. levels. When changes move forward without taking into account potential or actual resistance levels, the change can be negatively impacted. Whether it be an agency-wide Lean implementation or a team working on a Kaizen project event, it's extremely beneficial to do the work "up front" to identify the key stakeholders, discuss how they view the change, determine where they need to be to enhance the likelihood for success, and then to develop a strategic plan to get them there. This is done based on the team's best estimate of where the various stakeholders are positioned. Care must be taken to treat this document in confidence among team members. A "public sharing' of the document should be done by concealing the real stakeholder groups or individuals with "coded" names; otherwise there could be some sensitivity problems.

A Stakeholder is any person or group of people who:
* Are likely to be affected, positively or negatively, by the Change Initiative.
* Are in a position to assist or block achievement of the outcomes.
* Are experts or special resources that could substantially affect the quality of the end product/service.
* Can have influence over other stakeholders.

Identify those individuals with an interest in the process and what their positions on a particular Change Initiative might be.

A Stakeholder Analysis should be utilized when a Lean Government initiative is in the beginning stages to try to anticipate all stakeholder groups to better plan for success. For example, Government stakeholders can include: employees, citizens/taxpayers, outside agencies, state and federal Government, advocacy groups, city councils, unions, media, suppliers, commissions, and others. A Stakeholder Analysis should also be utilized for any major projects, Kaizen events, or significant changes. It is an excellent way to create the basis for a communications strategy.

Steps:

1. Brainstorm key stakeholders by individual or group name or title. Plot where they currently are with regard to desired change (X = current).
2. Plot where they need to be at the minimum level (O = desired) in order to successfully accomplish desired change. Identify the gaps between current and desired levels.
3. Plan action steps for closing gaps with influence strategy.
4. Who influences other Stakeholders?

Stakeholder Analysis

Stakeholder Name	Strongly Against -2	Moderately Against -1	Neutral 0	Moderately Supportive +1	Strongly Supportive +2	Type of Resistance	Plan to Address
A				X/O			Elevator Speech - Mayor's Newsletter
B				X/O			Elevator Speech - Chamber meeting
C			X ⟶ O				Committee Meetings
D			X/O				OK as is
E		X ⟶			O		3PM Thursday Meeting - Kaizen report out
F		X ⟶		O			3PM Thursday Meeting - Kaizen report out
G		X ⟶			O		3PM Thursday Meeting - Kaizen report out
H			X ⟶ O				3PM Friday Meeting - Kaizen report out
I			X ⟶ O				3PM Friday Meeting - Kaizen report out
J				X/O			OK as is

Figure 3.5

In the example above (Figure 3.5), the stakeholder individual or group names are "protected". Consideration must be given whether openly disclosing or protecting stakeholders is the appropriate strategy. In some cases, the team may view that a significant shift must take place for a particular stakeholder, or stakeholder group, which must result in a specific strategy or actions to cause the shift to happen. Accountability for these actions must be assigned. As can be seen in the above example, in some cases the stakeholder's position is fine, hence no real action is required (other than perhaps, general communications, like the elevator speech). Stakeholder action plans can be elaborate if the change initiative is complex and/or involves a larger group.

Resistance must be assessed and dealt with through a variety of positive strategies to mitigate the resistance level (strategies vary depending on the source of the resistance), some examples are:

Education /Communications	Educate people about the change as soon as it is feasible and before it is implemented. Team meetings, 1:1 meetings, e-mails, etc. Clearly state the WIIFM (What's In It For Me). This can also involve more training.
Involvement/Participation	Have people involved in teams, committees, idea sessions, etc. to engage in the change
Coaching/Support	Provide help for individuals to cope with the change.

Authority	The change is going to happen and you need all team members on the "bus".
Political	Show why the change is not a "loss"and/or empathize with the loss.

WHY LEAN INITIATIVES FAIL (now for the bad news)

Sustainable success rates for Lean Management System implementations are low. Many estimates range from 5-15% sustainable success. If the Lean tools are easy to understand and do (next chapter), then why is there such a high failure rate? The overarching cause is a lack of leadership will and "all in" commitment. The following areas dominate the cause of failures:

1.Establishing a Sense of Urgency

- No sense of urgency created – no accountability.
- Absence of senior leadership.
- No commitment of leadership to understand change.
- Complacency rules the day.

2.Creating a Guiding Coalition

- Champions have poor positional power.
- No formal coalition established.
- Poor commitment to up-front workshops and training.
- No clear accountability for results.
- Guiding deployment with weak steering teams.
- Not weeding out people who are resisting change.

3.Developing a Vision and Strategy

- No vision has developed – program is a training program rather than an improvement initiative.
- Vision is not linked to strategy.
- No sense of urgency to support the vision.
- Lean not linked to strong results.
- Doing Lean to merely "check a box".

4.Communicating the Change Vision

- No communication plan – Lean becomes a stealth program.
- Communication at upper levels but not at lower levels.
- Leadership is not visible in the commitment and communication.
- Under-communicating ("…but I've already said it a hundred times).

5. Empowering Employees for Broad-based Action	7. Consolidating Gains and Producing More Change
• No leadership commitment to intense workshops and training (self or employees). • Little involvement in project selection. • No project tracking that's easily visible. • Lean viewed as a nice training program. • Little on-site project support given.	• Lean initiative stagnates. • Internal experts not developed. • Initiative results not carefully tracked via metrics. • Lean projects seen as extra work that detracts from day-to-day operations. • Convincing the organization that they are done when they are not.
6. Generating Short-term Wins	**8. Anchoring the New Approaches in the Culture**
• No accountability established. • More than 12 months to achieve reasonable results. • No formal recognition ceremonies with clear presence of senior leadership. • No clear financial support to establish business impact. • Launching too many projects at once. • Providing the first win too slowly.	• Business as usual – if Lean disappeared, no one would notice. • Promotions not linked to Lean activities. • No development of internal resources to support program. • Few changes in systems and leadership style. • Students consistently show up at training with poorly defined, small projects.

It's absolutely critical to have a change management strategy in place to minimize the resistance that will be encountered and maximize the ability to create a sustainable, successful, Lean Government initiative.

A survey in the American Society for Quality's (ASQ) spring, 2017, Government division newsletter[4] compiled the results and some of the findings of the people surveyed were:

• Lean is capable of producing substantial positive impact in Government. Of the projects surveyed there was an average 61% reduction in process steps, a 60% reduction in process time, and a 19% improvement in error-free work. Of the problem statements worked on, 54% were externally focused to improve the agency output, while 46% were internally focused on business problems within the agency.

• The barriers to success were:

- o The most significant was that employees are sensitive to the fact that making improvements will result in job losses and budget reductions.
- o Lack of support or lack of resources can prevent the realization of the proposed improvements.
- o Lack of a holistic organizational improvement focus. Mainly the organizations were focused on utilizing Lean tools.
- o A successful part of an agency has difficulty spreading Lean to other parts of the agency (lack of top management leadership).
- The key recommendations from the survey were:
  - o Government leaders everywhere should embrace Lean process improvement as an ongoing management strategy and as a required management practice.
  - o Executive leadership must create a safe and beneficial career transition for employees who work on process improvements that lead to the elimination of existing jobs. Executive leadership should allow agencies the freedom to repurpose the savings and apply to other areas to create greater capacity and service instead of reducing budgets. Layoffs should not be done. Attrition (and not replacing positions) is the best viable option when there are budgetary pressures.
  - o There should be a holistic strategic Lean approach as opposed to merely applying Lean tools.

CHAPTER SUMMARY: Lean Government is a major change initiative and change management strategies must be robustly applied to create a sustainable success. This means that actions, behaviors, systems and structures must all change to create a sustainable Lean Government model.

REFERENCES:

[1]Kotter, John P. (2012) *Leading Change*. Boston: Harvard Business Review Press Print. Kotter, John P. (2010) *Buy In.* Boston: Harvard Business Review Press Print.
[2]https://www.prosci.com/adkar/adkar-model
[3]Liker, Dr. Jeffrey (2004). *The Toyota Way*; McGraw-Hill.
[4]**Achievements and Barriers: The Results of Lean and Quality Initiatives in Government**. (Spring, 2017). ASQ Government Division Newsletter.

Chapter 4
Customers

Who are these people and what do they want or need?

Government employees labor away at processes that are very customer unfriendly, without seeing these processes from the eyes of the customer; unfortunately, this is not uncommon. It's also not the employees' fault as they work in a system and its associated processes. The customer has no choice who they have to do business with since the Government entity has no competitors. It's the only game in town.

A state agency responsible for regulating and reporting on natural gas and energy was beset with an overload of call center complaints about the unfair energy rates customers (citizens and businesses) felt they were being charged. Working with the agency, the first step was to see how easy it was for the customer to get the information they needed to address their issues.

Looking at the agency website as a first step was enlightening. How easy is it for customers to get their issues addressed? This agency's website had evolved and grown over time, making it more complex and difficult for a customer to obtain an answer. To get to an electronic form to file a complaint, the customer had to navigate through four separate computer drop down menu screens. Will customers take the time to do this? Most won't; they'll just call the agency. A website overhaul was needed, but how to design it was the question.

So, the place to start was to determine why customers were calling. What are the reasons (topics) for the calls, what is the call duration, how often are the calls dropped, how fast are the calls answered, etc.? A simple spreadsheet was set up for data collection. As it turned out, the #1 reason for customer calls (complaints) was customers felt they were being overcharged. The agency then was able to address this concern by placing the prevailing monthly energy costs on the main page of its website. Furthermore, the agency couldn't do anything about these complaints and shouldn't have been handling them in the first place! Next, a link to the phone numbers of all the energy service providers was provided with on the website. Customers could now see if their rates were out of line. It was then made clear that the first step customers had to take was to contact their energy provider. If they weren't satisfied with their energy provider's resolution of their complaint, the next step was to contact the agency. Once the customers' situation was understood, updating the website with rate and provider contact information resulted in a severe drop in calls and complaints. Once the number of complaints dropped, dropped calls decreased since customers were being answered the first time. In turn, this call center volume dropped by more than 60% in a span of three months.

Who are the customers of Government?

- Citizens

- Taxpayers (a subset of citizens, since many citizens don't pay taxes)

- Businesses

- Other Government agencies

- Government employees, including employee unions

- Advocacy groups

- Non-profits

- and the list goes on

What services do customers need?

Client needs are normally more vague and high level, such as *I need a quick response*. It's necessary to transmit this into more specific information, as an example, *I don't want to wait in line longer than 5 minutes*. Gathering the necessary information is known as the Voice of the Customer (VOC). It can't be assumed what customers need, there has to be a means of gathering information/data to develop a broader, deeper understanding of what these needs are.

A study done in Ontario, Canada in 2005[1] on what customers wanted from Government found the following (none of the findings are surprising):

The 5 Key Drivers of Government Client Satisfaction

Timeliness   I was satisfied with the amount of time it took to get good service.

Knowledge   Staff was knowledgeable and competent.

Extra Mile   Staff went the extra mile to get me what I wanted.

Fairness   I was treated fairly.

Outcome   In the end, I got what I needed.

The prioritized response rate for each factor was (total of 100% - Figure 4.1):

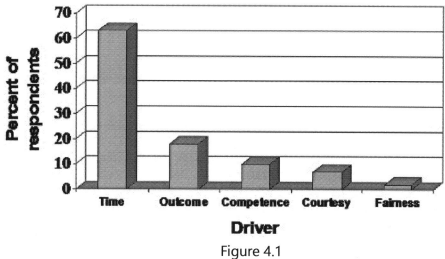

Figure 4.1

The survey then drilled down further to determine what specifics did citizens want (multiple individually rated customer answers):

Citizens Want	% response
Reduced waiting in lines, on the phone, in the mail, etc.	74%
Reduced Red Tape	68%
Create a "one-stop" service	68%
Simplify forms and documents	65%
Extend office hours	63%
Make it easier to get information about the service	62%
Use plain language	60%
Make the service available electronically	60%
Give more decision making power to the staff	53%

The Ontario, Canada example illustrates how one Government determined what their customers wanted from Government services. They set up a series of specific performance metrics for the public to see.

Each Government entity may arrive at some different wants and needs based on their Voice of the Customer (VOC) data. We need to ensure there is good customer information before the leap is made to creating unwanted solutions. We can't rely on inward, Government-driven solutions, when the solutions should be outward and customer-driven. There are many means of determining VOC needs information (see Figure 4.2 below):

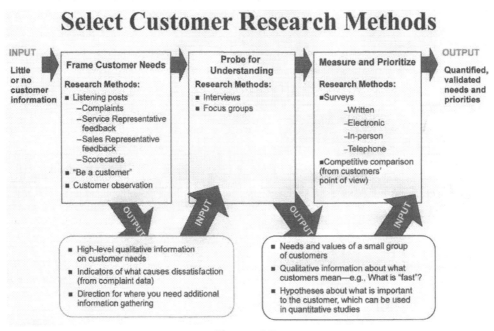

Figure 4.2

Given the situation, one or several, of these methods will yield quantified, validated customer needs information.

Another example was a state Motor Vehicle Department (DMV) with a four-person compliant department that was far behind in processing complaints. The first step was to look at the types/categories of complaints that were submitted to the agency by customers. Through a simple check sheet they were able to determine the type of complaints and frequency of occurrence.

They found that more than 50% of the complaints were related to car dealer and service station issues, which should not have been processed by the DMV. The customers should have been taking their complaints to their dealer and then small claims court for resolution. It was made clear on the DMV website that customers calling about dealer repair work should be redirected to the respective dealer first and small claims court next, if the customer wasn't satisfied. The resulting DMV complaint level dropped in excess of 50%. This freed up two employees to help out in other areas of the DMV.

Another Call Center Case Study

Government entities have numerous call centers to help customers get answers and/or resolve issues and problems. Automated computer answering systems, such as IVR (Interactive Voice Response), need to be continually tested for customer effectiveness. Call volume data abounds (time of day, duration of call, day of week, etc.), but is it the right data?

We need to know why people are calling. Call reasons need to be captured in a very consistent way by the call center staff. This combines the concepts of:

- Operational Definitions = call center personnel being able to consistently make the same determination of what type of call they've received.
- Repeatability and Reproducibility = will the same staff member receiving the call make the same determination each time (are they repeatable?) and between several staff members taking calls will they make the same determination between each other (this is known as reproducible).

Once accurate call center data is captured, then the data can be analyzed for the dominant call reasons, leading to determining the root causes. Root causes then lead to being able to try some corrective actions or countermeasures to eliminate or significantly reduce the root causes.

Figure 4.3 illustrates the effects of having good data and root cause analysis. The center started applying Lean data and root cause analysis in July. There was plenty of data that the call center was struggling with previously to make improvements, with no real success. Dropped calls were high due to customer frustration, which led to more calls. Once good data was captured with an effective root cause analysis, they better understood the types of calls and how to implement changes to improve the customer experience to either prevent the call (through better customer education), or handle the call more effectively. This also resulted in the reduction of temporary staff and overtime costs.

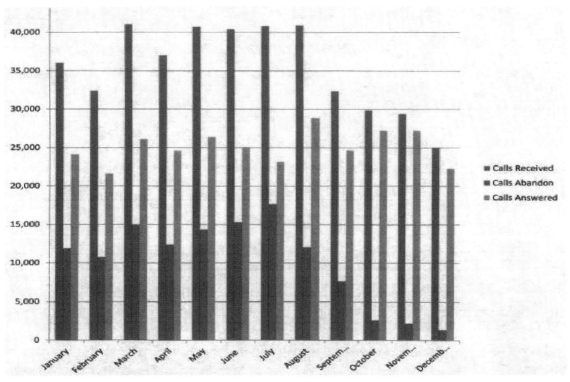

Figure 4.3

Communicate and educate customers:

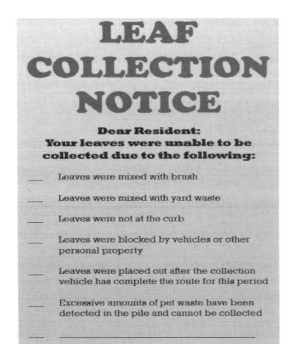

This is an example of a city that was having problems with residential leaf collection. They created a simple tag to explain why the leaves couldn't be picked up and left the notice on the customer's door. Customers were educated and other customers saw the notices and also learned. Leaf removal teams carried this notice along with other notices to be dispensed on the spot.

Reduce the complexity in any paperwork the customer has to fill out

When there is no time available to review and see what current customer paperwork exists, more gets added, along with greater complexity. This leads to greater customer confusion and frustration, which leads to increasing error rates and internal staff rework rates. Having good data on customer errors and rework leads to identifying the root causes and then the corrective actions to try.

Some guidelines for good forms design:
- Call to actions should be clear and as early as possible.
- Clarity is paramount – operational definitions – if you can't answer with greater consistency/less variation, evaluate why it is in the form and/or make it clearer.
- Minimize unnecessary words and use more checklists.
- Use font sizes, white spaces, shading and/or colors to distinguish areas and create separation – make the form more visual and easier to navigate.
- Determine order/sequence/format – what should be first, second, etc.?
- Set up forms based on data – the worst data response areas (causing errors and rework) should be placed earlier in the form.
- Cover acronym definitions.

Expand the use of checklists and reduce or eliminate long wordy documents. Also make the checklists visual – put in pictures and number the sequence of how things should be filled out.

The rationale for using checklists:
- Extreme complexity and specialization lead to difficulty remembering the routine tasks.
- It is easy to overlook routine tasks under the strain of other demands on attention (especially high stress).
- It is easy to skip steps even when you remember them - it doesn't matter until it does.
- They ensure that people consistently apply their knowledge and expertise they have.
- They promote teamwork and learning as the checklist is improved with successive uses.
- They strike a balance between professional judgment and protocol.

Here is an example of going from a poor, complex instruction form to an easy one page checklist:

Go from this (8 pages of instruction): To this (1 page checklist):

PLEASE READ CAREFULLY BEFORE COMPLETING YOUR IRP RENEWAL. RENEWALS WILL BE RETURNED IF ITEMS NEEDED ARE MISSING OR THE RENEWAL IS NOT COMPLETED CORRECTLY.

UPDATE YOUR USDOT NUMBER INFORMATION WITHIN 12 MONTHS OF YOUR IRP REGISTRATION EXPIRATION DATE: If your USDOT number information, or the USDOT number information of the motor carrier you may be leased onto, has not been updated within 12 months of your registration expiration date, a pre-printed MCS-150 form for each USDOT number not currently updated will be included in your renewal package. You may manually update your USDOT number information in RED INK on the pre-printed MCS-150 form with the updated mileage and year in section 22 and sign the MCS-150 form on page two. Only an authorized person of the motor carrier you may be leased onto can update and sign the pre-printed MCS-150 form for their USDOT number. Return all updated and signed MCS-150 forms with your renewal. Or, you may electronically update your USDOT number information online at www.safer.fmcsa.dot.gov. Click on "Registration & Licensing" to proceed with online update of your USDOT number information. You, and the motor carrier you may be leased onto, must provide a federal Employer's Identification Number (EIN). (Connecticut does not accept a Social Security Number in place of a federal EIN). To obtain a no-charge federal EIN, call the Internal Revenue Services at 1-800-829-4933. Your IRP apportioned registration(s) will not be renewed until you, and the motor carrier you may be leased onto, have provided a federal EIN with updated USDOT number information.

IF YOU DO NOT WISH TO RENEW, write "NOT RENEWING" across the renewal application, sign and date and return the Renewal Schedules B and A/E with your APPORTIONED plates and cabcard(s) to the IRP Unit, Room 260, 60 State Street, Wethersfield, CT 06161-1010 when the current registration(s) expire. All APPORTIONED plates are the property of the State of Connecticut, and must be returned ONLY to the IRP Unit in Wethersfield.

IF YOU WISH TO RENEW, complete the enclosed Renewal Schedules B and A/E. Verify all information printed on the applications, and make any necessary changes or corrections using RED INK. Renewals completed in pencil will be returned. Write the ACTUAL mileage data (DO NOT ROUND OFF) next to each jurisdiction which you traveled in during the mileage reporting period as indicated on Renewal Schedule B, in Instruction B. Write ESTIMATED mileages next to the jurisdictions which you want to add to your account, or which you want to maintain in your account although no ACTUAL mileage was accrued in the jurisdictions during the mileage reporting period. To provide ESTIMATED mileages for any jurisdiction, use the enclosed (blue) ESTIMATED MILEAGE SCHEDULE and provide a detailed reason for estimating mileage.

MAIL YOUR RENEWAL APPLICATIONS IN THE ENCLOSED RETURN ENVELOPE AT LEAST 45 DAYS BEFORE YOUR REGISTRATION EXPIRATION DATE. After we do the computations based on the mileage data and vehicles you listed on Renewal Schedules B and A/E, we will MAIL you the invoice with the amount you must pay for renewal. Return the ORIGINAL invoice and if additional information is noted on the invoice enclose with payment in GUARANTEED FUNDS (certified check, money order, or bank check) at least 15 days before your registration expiration date. Upon receipt of payment in guaranteed funds, we will MAIL to you your renewed registration cabcard(s) listing jurisdictions of travel, and your windshield expiration sticker(s). We will also mail plates, if you added vehicles.

**INTERNATIONAL REGISTRATION PLAN (IRP)
RENEWAL DOCUMENTS
USER CHECKLIST**

IF you are NOT renewing your IRP Account, write "NOT RENEWING" across the Renewal Schedules B and A sign and date and return - with your Apportioned IRP plates and cabcards - when current registrations(s) expire

___ ACORD CERTIFICATE OF LIABILITY INSURANCE (see Enclosure A), with:

___ An INSURED business address that is the same as the name on the IRP Account

___ The CERTIFICATE HOLDER as:

___ A POLICY NUMBER

___ Current POLICY EFFECTIVE/EXPIRATION DATES

___ An INSURED name that is the same as the Registrant Name on the IRP Account (and is the same as the name of the "Owner of Vehicle" on IRP Schedule A/E)

___ An AUTOMOBILE LIABILITY COMBINED SINGLE LIMIT of at least $750,000

___ If AUTOMOBILE LIABILITY is ANY AUTO (Blanket Policy), individual vehicles DO NOT need to be listed

___ If AUTOMOBILE LIABILITY is ALL OWNED VEHICLES, SCHEDULED AUTOS, HIRED AUTOS and NON-OWNED AUTOS ALL vehicles must be listed by Year, Make and Vehicle Identification Number (VIN)

___ If "Leased On" to a motor carrier, the INSURED name must include the name of the motor carrier AND the Lessor information must be included under DESCRIPTION OF OPERATIONS/LOCATIONS/VEHICLES/EXCLUSIONS ADDED BY ENDORSEMENT/SPECIAL PROVISIONS

___ If "Leased On" to a motor carrier, proof of Bobtail or Non-Trucking Liability Insurance

___ COPY/COPIES OF THE CURRENT DRIVER'S LICENSE(S) OF THE CONTACT PERSON(S) ON IRP SCHEDULE B

___ Current SECRETARY OF THE STATE (SOTS) BUSINESS FILING (or copies of the Filing Application and the check submitted to the Secretary of the State)

___ Copy of IRS HEAVY VEHICLE USE TAX (HVUT) 2290 receipt for the current tax period for all vehicles 55,000 pounds or more gross vehicle weight

___ Copy, if applicable, of UNIFIED CARRIER REGISTRATION (UCR) payment

___ IRP SCHEDULE B (RENEWAL APPLICATION) completed in ink, with:
___ If Estimated Miles listed, the reason(s)

A CHECKLIST FOR CHECKLISTS

Development → Drafting → Validation

Development	Drafting	Validation
❏ Do you have clear, concise objectives for your checklist?	**Does the Checklist:** ❏ Utilize natural breaks in workflow (pause points)? ❏ Use simple sentence structure and basic language? ❏ Have a title that reflects its objectives? ❏ Have a simple, uncluttered, and logical format? ❏ Fit on one page? ❏ Minimize the use of color?	**Have you:** ❏ Trialed the checklist with front line users (either in a real or simulated situation)? ❏ Modified the checklist in response to repeated trials?
Is each item: ❏ A critical safety step and in great danger of being missed? ❏ Not adequately checked by other mechanisms? ❏ Actionable, with a specific response required for each item? ❏ Designed to be read aloud as a verbal check? ❏ One that can be affected by the use of a checklist?	**Is the font:** ❏ Sans serif? ❏ Upper and lower case text? ❏ Large enough to be read easily? ❏ Dark on a light background?	**Does the checklist:** ❏ Fit the flow of work? ❏ Detect errors at a time when they can still be corrected? ❏ Can the checklist be completed in a reasonably brief period of time? ❏ Have you made plans for future review and revision of the checklist?
Have you considered: ❏ Adding items that will improve communication among team members? ❏ Involving all members of the team in the checklist creation process?	❏ Are there fewer than 10 items per pause point? ❏ Is the date of creation (or revision) clearly marked?	Gawande[2]

CHAPTER SUMMARY - LESSONS LEARNED SERVICING CUSTOMERS:

1. "Be the customer" – Step back and see what you have to do if you were a customer interfacing with your agency or department. What information do customers need and how easy is it to find? What are the most frequent reasons for customer contact or complaints? Why are we doing what we're doing? Over time and the passing of knowledge to others, have we lost our way and are now doing things that aren't necessary? Is employee retraining required?
2. Don't assume what the customer wants or needs – go and obtain the factual data from customers before proceeding. You may get a surprise!
3. Design information and instructions for customers – many Government websites and forms have gone through the legal departments and are at the college reading level. The New York Times is at the 10th grade reading level. The average citizen is at the 7th grade reading level. Design customer information at the appropriate reading level and with the forms' design guidelines in mind.

REFERENCES:

[1]Citizens First 4 report, 2005. Phase 5 Consulting Group Inc., for the ICCS and Institute of Public Administration of Canada, page 23.
[2]Gawande, Atul, (2009). *The Checklist Manifesto: How to Get Things Right.* Metropolitan Books.

Chapter 5
Benchmarking

How to steal shamelessly, but legally

Benchmarking is the opportunity to find best practices and to learn and adapt from others to save your organization from reinventing the wheel. It's important to do as part of any problem solving effort. Based on its discoveries, benchmarking also allows the internal team to determine what others are doing and raise the starting point for improving the process to a much higher level. What you learn can then become the baseline for further improvement. This eliminates waste -- spending time creating something that has already been developed, tested and improved by another organization. Before launching a process improvement project, it is important to first determine if benchmarking should, in fact, be done. It's much easier to do in Government since there is minimal competition; however, in our experience working with Government, benchmarking is underutilized. For example, an economic development department in Dallas could benefit from talking to Atlanta or Seattle to determine best practices before beginning any process improvement project.

In Government, benchmarking processes such as accounts payable, procurement, tax collection, public works services, hiring new people and customer complaints are the most common forms. The purpose is to identify the best operating processes and procedures with benchmark partners. Other areas that can be benchmarked are performance (how do others perform with customers – time to produce a document, error rates, how fast phone calls are returned, etc.), or strategic and planning approaches.

DeKalb County, GA, embarked on a Kaizen event to address water meter reading and billing accuracy. The first benchmarking effort was to ask other Government entities if they had worked on improving a similar process and also obtain information about their current process. Another benchmarking effort was to determine how other entities handled property liens when owners had violations (Figure 5.1).

Benchmarking created a baseline to compare DeKalb County with its counterparts so they could then focus on further improvement efforts to create a better future state process.

DeKalb County
Treasury & Accounting
LIEN PROCESS COMPARISON

	AMOUNT LIENABLE	SERVICE ON/OFF	INTENT LETTER	PAYMENT ARRANGEMENTS	COLLECTIONS	SURETY BONDS	COMMENTS
CITY OF ATLANTA	OVER $300.00	OFF	YES	NO	YES	NO	
COBB COUNTY	$50.00	OFF	YES	YES	YES	YES	
DOUGLAS COUNTY	DOES NOT LIEN	OFF			YES	NO	STARTS COLLECTION PROCESS
FORSYTHE COUNTY, NC	ANY	OFF	YES	NO	YES	NO	
ROCKDALE COUNTY	DOES NOT LIEN						
FULTON COUNTY	ANY	OFF	?	NO	NO	NO	LIEN OWNERS FROM DISCONNECT
GWINNETT COUNTY	$250.00	ON	YES	YES	YES	NO	COLLECTIONS START 60 DAYS
NEWTON COUNTY	DOES NOT LIEN	OFF			YES		
HENRY COUNTY	YES						
CITY OF AUSTELL	$500.00	OFF	YES	YES	YES	NO	
DEKALB COUNTY	$1,000.00	ON/OFF	YES	YES	NO	NO	

Figure 5.1

In Westlake, OH, the Kaizen team was working on a Request for Services/Work Order Process. They were not satisfied with the public works work order software. The easy solution would have been to just go out and buy a new software package. Instead, they opted first to benchmark two areas:

1. How were work orders being handled by others? Three similar-sized Ohio cities were selected to benchmark. The team developed a simple question form which they sent via email (after a heads-up call) to the key counterpart in each city beforehand and then followed up with a conference call the following day. (Figure 5.2):

1 How do you track and manage service/work requests for work in your department?

_____
_____
_____

   A. How do you pass off requests that do not pertain to your department?

   _____
   _____
   _____

2 Who enters or captures that information?

_____
_____

Figure 5.2

   A. How many people are involved with entering the information?

   _____
   _____
   _____

   B. Who do the service requests come from?

   _____
   _____
   _____

   C. What are the initial points of contacts? i.e. staff members, councilpeople, etc.

   _____
   _____

Another outcome of benchmarking was that each of the cities was able to learn from each other to make collective work order system gains. It was a win-win for everyone.

2. The team also decided to review the websites of the same three cities to see how easy it was for the customer to navigate the city website for information on how to initiate and determine the status of public works work orders. The Westlake team found that the other cities made it much easier for customers to navigate websites and that they also used Facebook, Twitter, and Instagram as part of their social media strategy. These findings created the impetus for Westlake to initiate an effort to upgrade its website.

There have been numerous instances where benchmarking has identified processes or process steps that an agency, city, county or school is doing that their benchmarked counterparts don't feel even need to be done. This is a pure form of waste – eliminate doing the unnecessary and make the process better!

A social services agency worked on improving its protective services process for the elderly. This included how to make assessments with less social worker variation and determining the appropriate response level for social workers based on the situations that confronted their elder clients. There were several response levels based on the severity of the situation. The most urgent response level (imminent life threatening) initially had the team working on approaches to improve that level of the process, while other levels took more of a back seat. A simple benchmarking exercise determined that no other comparable agency in other states responded to this level. The benchmark approach was to refer the situation to the 911 emergency responder networks. This was an excellent example of benchmarking pointing out an unnecessary process step before the team invested time in improving that step.

There are several broad categories which can be effectively utilized for benchmarking:
- Generic Comparisons: Learning more about improving call center operations can involve many different non-Government organizations.
- Similar function comparisons: Benchmark other similar Government organizations. The size of the organization may or may not be an area for consideration.
- Competitor comparisons: Neighboring states or cities, for example, may have economic development incentives to benchmark.
- Internal comparisons: For example, one school in a large school district of 50 schools may do certain processes very well.
- Trade publications: Read articles and contact the author.
- Membership in professional associations: Inquiries can be made via association networking sites.
- The internet: Information can be Googled. Use internet sites such as *Linked In Groups* to make inquiries or search for topics of interest.

An accounts payable example illustrates some benchmarking questions to ask:
- Review process steps for specific activities (e.g., How are vendors paid?).
- Review related cost for specific activities (e.g., How much does it cost to pay a single vendor?).
- Ask others if they are willing to share related times for specific activities (e.g., How much time does it typically take to process a single payment?).
- Review information related to the quality of a particular activity. (e.g., On average, how many errors do you see? Rework levels? How did you reduce errors and improve quality?).
- If jurisdictions have conducted Kaizen events, questions related to how they quantified the benefits of their Kaizen events can be useful.

Take a Plan-Do-Check-Act approach to benchmarking (Chapter7, Problem Solving, page 101)
Plan – Analyze your internal process, select the subject of focus, define the process and identify potential partners. The benchmarking team must have some training.
Do – Develop the questionnaire, conduct the benchmark study (prepare and conduct the survey) and capture the relevant information/data.
Check – Review the results, analyze the gaps and determine the best practices.
Act – Create the strategy and implement the findings to improve the current process. Monitor the results and adjust accordingly. Provide feedback to the benchmark partners.

Robert C. Camp, the founding father of benchmarking when he was at Xerox in the early 1980's, developed a sequence of steps for benchmarking[1]:

1. **Select the subject of focus**. What process do you want to benchmark and why? How do you measure your current performance? What is the target process goal? Doing benchmarking should be a given before doing any internal process improvement work. Find out if you're doing the unnecessary.

2. **Define the process.** Use clear definitions of what you're trying to achieve for your benchmarking partners – you don't want to waste their time going back and forth trying to understand what you're trying to do.

3. **Identify potential partners.** Select partners and collect data. Use like-sized cities (in Westlake's case), professional organizations (for larger K-12 schools it could be the Council of Great City Schools), or even be a partner in a totally different field (call center operations are also in private sector companies). Decide how you're going to gather the information.
   - Who would be the best person or group to contact at the benchmark partner? Prepare background information and do research on the partner beforehand. .
   - Develop a survey form and send it electronically (i.e. Survey Monkey)
   - Conduct a conference call.
   - Do an on-site visit (most costly to do for all involved).

4. **Identify data sources**. Ask if your benchmark partner has data on the process and what type of data is available. This is helpful to have beforehand along with sharing with your benchmark partner how you measure the process and your data.

5. **Establish process differences and determine the gap.** What is the gap between your process current state and your benchmark partner? What process improvements can you make to close the gap and adapt or adopt what your benchmark partner is doing? Closing the gap creates a new current state process which is the springboard to an even better future state process. Closing the process gap to create a new current state may result in a new process that meets the internal stated needs or goals and would become a lesser priority. Improvement efforts need to continue to be focused on areas that create the greatest leverage. Improvement areas that have good impact, coupled with a worthwhile effort to implement, should be done.

6. **Target future performance and adjust the goal.** Establish the new process goal. Does it meet current needs? Benchmarking has established a new current state and a determination needs to be made if further improvement efforts are warranted. The future state goal should be updated. Does the process need further effort from the new baseline established as a result of the benchmarking?

7. **Communicate.** All appropriate stakeholders should be communicated with about the benchmarking outcome, plans and implemented results.

8. **Implement** – Put the desired improvements in place, monitor the results and make any further improvement adjustments.

CHAPTER SUMMARY - BENCHMARKING: All major improvement projects should have a benchmarking component as part of the improvement process (Kaizen events, etc.). Benchmarking requires management commitment and support. It's also relevant for solving specific problems.

REFERENCES:

[1]Camp, Robert C. (1994). *Benchmarking*; Hanser.

REFERENCE MATERIALS FOR FURTHER READING ON BENCHMARKING:

Also, good sources for benchmarking information are a variety of professional organizations such as:
- American Productivity and Quality Center (APQC)- an excellent site: https://www.apqc.org/benchmarking
- National Governors Association (NGA)
- International City/County Management Association (ICMA)
- Government Finance Officers Association (GFOA)
- Council of Great City Schools (CGCS)
- And many others

Chapter 6
Eliminating Waste

"Over 94% of what is done is waste." Dr. W. Edwards Deming

In our experience, when you consider all forms of process waste, we have seen some processes with in excess of 99% waste. In Government, much of this is waiting time. That is why it is important to ensure everyone is able to relentlessly identify and remove waste, particularly since there are degrees of overlap as one waste can impact another.

There are many forms of waste that can be removed, thereby improving process effectiveness and efficiency. All employees should be trained and become proficient in identifying and removing waste. First, however, it is important to understand the concept of what adds value.

Value-Adding Activities – These activities transform materials and information into programs and services the customer wants or needs and it is done right the first time.

Non-Value-Adding Activities (WASTE or MUDA) – These activities consume resources but do not directly contribute to a program or service and the customer doesn't care or want to pay for these activities. These process steps must be eliminated.

Value-Enabling Activities – These activities are those that must be done to support value-added activities and ensure they have been completed properly, but don't necessarily add any value. Some legislation may fall into value enabling – it has to be done, but it doesn't add any value.

Figure 6.1 depicts the various forms of waste:

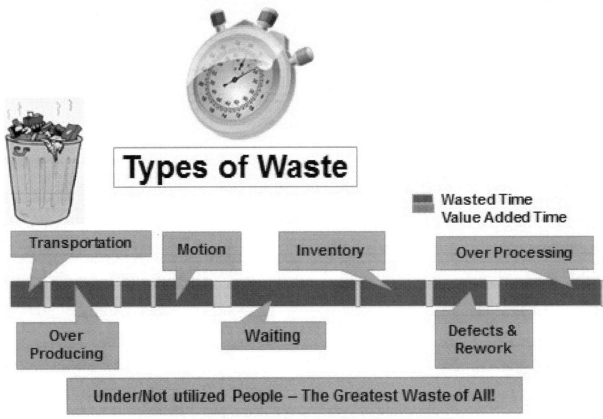

Figure 6.1

The acronyms are a way to easily remember the eight forms of wastes:

TIMWOOD-U	DOWNTIME
Transportation	Defects & Rework
Inventory	Over Producing
Motion	Waiting
Waiting	Not Utilizing Employee Inputs
Over Producing	Transportation
Over Processing	Inventory
Defects & Rework	Motion
Under-utilized employees	Extra Processing

A work area visible display on waste:

Here is a review of each of the wastes with some Government-related examples:

1. **TRANSPORTATION:** Areas of transportation waste can include:
- Moving documents, forms, etc., between work areas, offices, floors, buildings, etc. – an example would be interoffice mail or approvals
- Research requiring multiple department forwarding and cycling
- Requiring customers to go to various departments or agencies
- Large distances between process steps – poor process flow
- Large centralized file storage areas to access (more and more is becoming electronic)
- Physically travelling when a phone call would have sufficed

When working with a state Administrative Services agency, it was discovered that one of their key processes had the two key units working in the same large building with one-tenth of a mile between them. These units were set up in their current locations based on space availability. Not only did it take time to walk between the units (on average 3-4 times per day), but it also added time taken having side conversations with non-process-related individuals during the walk. A central file storage area for key records was located in one unit, which caused more walking time to retrieve key records. The agency had also purchased several expensive centralized biz hub printing centers (high speed copying, printing, binding, fax); in effect, this contributed to waste as employees walked to pick up printed materials only to find that someone had already taken the material off the unit and misplaced the output. The result, once the data and flow charts were presented, was an office reorganization; both units were consolidated into one office area, with reduced waste and significantly improved productivity.

A good way to look at transportation is to actually draw a work flow map. This is an example from the City of Hartford tax payment process (Figure 6.2), which was the first client we worked with over 12 years ago (remember – there was less computerization then):

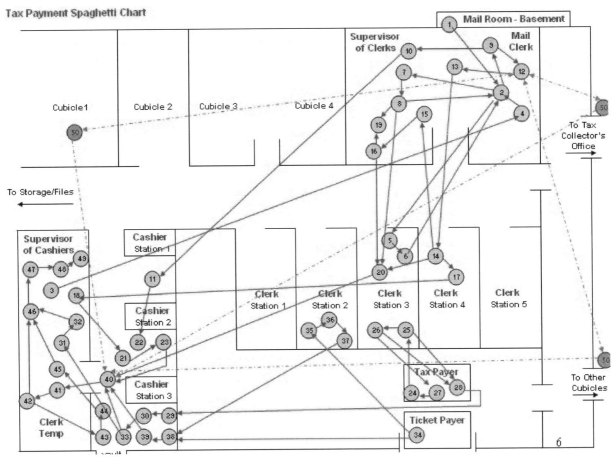

Figure 6.2

The main point of this example is to see the flow and transportation that took place to move the transaction through the system. In this case, there was more manual moving of the tax payment, whereas today, it would be mainly electronic. This mapping of the flow of the current state process helps highlight waste and is known as a "spaghetti map," since when most processes are mapped the lines on the map look like spaghetti!

Lessons learned identifying transportation waste:
First, obtain a physical floor or area process map. It could be within a building or within the city,

county or school district. Plot the transportation path for internal employees, customers or other stakeholders and determine how much of this waste can be eliminated. Options include: moving areas closer together, consolidating functions into one department, consolidating job categories to have fewer people touch the process, or other options.

2. **INVENTORY:** Areas of inventory waste can include:
- Making bulk purchases to get a "better deal" and storing the excess materials and, perhaps, throwing them away in the future due to obsolescence
- Filing and storing multiple copies of reports or documents in various locations
- Too much work in the "in" basket
- Accumulating work so it can be processed in batch mode. An example would be grouping categories of invoices together and processing them all at once, while other invoices are held up.
- Too much inventory causing too much clutter, making it harder to find what you need
- Record retention policies haven't been adhered to, leading to documents in various rental storage areas when the materials should have been legally disposed of earlier.

5S – ALTHOUGH LISTED UNDER INVENTORY, 5S HAS FAR BROADER IMPLICATIONS:

5S addresses minimizing many of the eight wastes. Its main benefit is being able to find what you need quickly while addressing many forms of waste. In an organization first embarking on a Lean journey, 5S is the easiest Lean tool to implement, but what is 5S? 5S was incorporated first in Japan and then adopted elsewhere.

S	Japanese Version	English Version
1	Seiri	Sort
2	Seiton	Set in Order
3	Seiso	Shiny Clean
4	Seiketsu	Standardize
5	Shitsuke	Sustain
6	Safety - Integrated throughout the 5S's	Safety

While 5S (6S with Safety) is easy for everyone to understand, excellent organization discipline and training is required for successful implementation. As always, a long-term holding the gains strategy is a challenge. The main outcome is finding things quickly freeing up time and physical resources, which leads to increases in personal and team productivity.

A Federal agency client started their 5S approach with a three-day session that kicked off with a three-hour training session on 5S and visual controls. The remainder of the three days was spent in the actual work areas, applying the 5S principles and making physical changes. This was applied across a 500+ employee maintenance department which serviced a large campus of 50+ buildings and 15,000+ total employees. The training was done once a month with 30 employees per three-day session. Over a three-month period (30 employees each month), 90 employees were trained and applied 5S to their work areas. The estimated productivity gain after the initial three-month period was 18%, with more than $2 million freed up from excess maintenance materials. Excess office furniture items were repurposed to other buildings, avoiding the need to order new items. The labor savings were achieved by being able to find "stuff" (perhaps this should be the 7th S?) quickly. Quickly means that an individual should be able to find an item in his/her area within 30 seconds while someone else entering the area should be able to find an item within 60 seconds. The freed up time was utilized to train employees to perform more value added maintenance work, saving on outside contractor costs. This emphasizes one of the key principles of Lean: employees shouldn't lose their jobs as a result of improvements.

Why do 5(6) S?
- Find things quickly and eliminate wastes from uncontrolled processes. It establishes a "visual workplace".
- Gain control of equipment, supplies, materials and inventory.
- Apply control techniques to eliminate the erosion of improvements.
- Standardize improvements in all work areas. 5S is especially impactful for areas that do maintenance work and have vehicles (especially public works departments):
  - Improve delivery consistency of services
  - Improve quality
  - Improve safety
  - Improve productivity
  - Everyone feels better about their workplace

The First S = Sort
Definition: To remove all items that are not required to do the current job. This also includes having items closer to the work area based on frequency of need/use. If you don't use it, get rid of it (legally!).

The first place to start is to assess the current state. It's extremely helpful to take "before" pictures for later reference and for employee education purposes. Individuals and organizations are pack rats when it comes to keeping items and not throwing anything away.

An actual city building department engineer's office (Figure 6.3 - before Sort):

Figure 6.3

Criteria:
- Distinguish between what is needed and not needed – eliminate what is not needed/
- Store often used items closer to the work area – the more frequent an item is used, the closer it should be.
- For safety purposes, heavier items should be stored to minimize the risk of injury (example: not on the top shelf or bottom shelf).

Benefits:
- Removes waste, making things easier and faster to find
- Safer work area
- Easier to visualize the process
- Frees up extra cabinets, racks, carts, storage containers that could find other uses and save procurement costs
- Improves space utilization:

A state agency mail room example of Sort (Figure 6.4):

Before Sort: After Sort:

Figure 6.4

It's obvious that all of the items that were stored had accumulated over a long period of time. When going through Sort, it was determined that none of the items were needed.

An example from a city economic development office (Figure 6.5) finding unnecessary materials during sort:

Figure 6.5

Because of all the excess materials, there was too much clutter. Finding the items necessary to do the job took more time.

Tips for Success:
- Observe all Environmental, Health & Safety guidelines.
- Start in one area, and then sort through everything.
- Discuss removal of items with all persons involved.
- Items that can't be removed immediately should be red tagged.
- Use movers and riggers, if necessary.
- Determine measures to prevent accumulation of that which is unnecessary.
- Know the specific record retention requirements and challenge anything that exceeds the timeframe.

Disposition Rules as you sort:
- Used at least once/day – return to the place of use in the work area
- Used once/week – store nearby
- Used once/month – store in an accessible area in the facility (on wheels, shelving, central area, etc.)
- Used once a year – store off site or rent
- No longer used – sell, auction, give away or throw out (legally)

The Red Tag Approach to dispose of unwanted items:
- Each participant attaches red tags to items that appear to be unnecessary.
  - Name, date, and why the red tag
- Remove tagged items to a holding area.
  - Items will remain in holding area for a period of time (1-2 weeks). People can view items and arrange to have them removed from the holding area to a designated area within this period via disposition rules. Everyone gets a chance to make sure the disposition is proper.
- Identify requirements for red tag items.
  - Define what is needed vs. what is not needed.
- Items that are no longer necessary: Inventory, machines and equipment, shelves, cabinets, files, desks, tools, etc.

An example of a Red Tag holding area (Figure 6.6):

Figure 6.6

Sort Reminders:
- Take before and after pictures
- Sort to a logical sequence
  - o Frequency of use – the more often, the closer
  - o Safety – heaviest materials in the position for greatest safety consideration
  - o Place in a logical sequence – for example, drill bits: ¼, 3/8, ½, etc.
- Red Tags – ensure all members of an area understand the red tag concept and that everyone needs to participate to decide on disposition.
  - o Ensure everyone knows what to do with Red Tag items – salvage, trash, auction, recycle, or...?

The Second S = Set in Order or Straighten

Definition: To arrange items that are needed in the area and identify/label them so that anyone can find them or put them back where they belong.

It's the old adage: "a place for everything and everything in its place." In a stockroom example, labeling is done with pictures, colors and numbers to make it easier to find items.

Note the use of bar codes labels on the inside of the doors (Figure 6.7). Other examples include taping the forms on the outside of the cabinet door exactly where they're located inside, making for easy access and searching.

Figure 6.7

Criteria:
- To arrange all necessary items
- A place for everything and everything in its place

Benefits:
- Visually shows what is required and what is out of place
- Makes it easy for anyone to find, use and return items
- Saves time, not having to search for items
- Shorter travel distances
- Know when it's time to reorder items

Tips for Success:
- Things that are used together are kept together in the sequence in which they are used.
- Use labels, tape, floor markings, signs, shadow outlines, etc.
- Keep shared items at a central location (eliminate excess).
- Determine how many of each item needs to be stored at each location.
- Use standard equipment.
- Take pictures of how the area is supposed to look and post prominently.

Figure 6.8 is an example from the city of Boca Raton, Florida, city clerk's office. Everything is labeled in clear plastic containers (a good start with some refinements still to be done to make the area even more visual and make items easier to find):

Figure 6.8

Use a Visual *Color* System for easy location of items:
- Utilization of colored lines and markers to indicate unique location areas and functions
- Area sub-divider lines
- Entrances and exits
- Direction and flow (different color lines on the floor to follow associated with how to get to different customer services)
- Location markers, work areas, walkways, rest areas, equipment locations, storage locations, etc.

Reminders:
- Clearly label shelves, units, etc., initially with masking tape and clear bold lettering – ask others in the area to review and modify locations to make the most sense. Start with PowerPoint paper signs; once locations are finalized, lock in with more permanent marking.
- Use a Home Depot or supermarket approach to aisles, floor maps, laminated locator sheets, pictures, numbers, colors, etc.

The Third S – Shine (Cleanliness)
Definition: To keep the workplace area clean and neat so any abnormalities/issues can be immediately identified. A well-lit and clean area also minimizes safety issues. A clean work area also leads to better employee morale.

Criteria:
- Keep the areas clean on a continuing basis, by continually keeping the workplace swept and wiped down and eliminating dirt, dust, oil, scrap and other foreign matter.

Benefits:
- Prevent the area from getting dirty in the first place, so there is no need to clean it up at a later time.
- A clean work environment is indicative of a quality service, product and process.
- Help identify equipment problems.
- Minimize/eliminate potential health problems by minimizing/eliminating dust and dirt.

Tips for Success:
- Adopt cleaning as a form of inspection. (Cleaning exposes abnormal conditions and corrects potential unsafe conditions.)
- Integrate cleaning into everyday maintenance tasks by all employees. (Cleaning builds value for equipment and pride in work areas.)
- Sweep / Vacuum, Dust / Mop, Polish / Paint
- Use good visual controls: Photograph and post how the area is supposed to look.

Reminders:
- Clean the area daily – everyone should be challenged to pick up in their area.
- Assign responsibility for clean-up – prominently post a daily sign off list.

The Fourth S – Standardize – Use Visual Controls
Definition: Explains the best way tasks should be performed.

Criteria: To thoroughly maintain and monitor the first 3S's - Sort, Straighten, and Shine.

Figure 6.9

This is an example (Figure 6.9) of a Motor Vehicle Department workstation set up based on the 5S layout; a visual control picture is in the area (circled) to ensure compliance. The more that pictures, colors and numbers are used, the better. Standardization is the utilization of best work practices consistently by everyone in the work area. This is "owned" by supervision with ownership also transferred to the employees in the area. Ensuring standards are maintained requires periodic random audits by supervisors or employees in the work area who have had the proper guidance and training. Audits are utilized to identify areas where there are deviations from the standards, to help understand the root causes of these deviations, and use our learnings from the root causes to further educate everyone in the area as to what happened and what corrective actions can be taken to prevent recurrences. This is part of the cycle of continuous improvement.

Benefits:
- Prevents regression to an unclean/disorganized environment (return items where they belong)
- Eliminates the need for "Special Clean-Up Efforts" (clean while the task is small - done daily)
- Easier to train new employees
- Less room for errors, rework and scrap
- Work area is safer and more organized

Tips for Success:
- Devise methods to maintain adherence to this state and prevent deviations from standards in order to:
  - Prevent accumulation
  - Ensure everything is returned to its own place
  - Maintain cleanliness standards - "Clean up after yourself"
- Standardize everything and make standards visible so that all abnormalities can be easily recognized.

- Develop schedules/checklists.

Reminders- Pictures, large and in colors, along with pictures of the employees who own the area, should be posted on how the areas should look.

Approaches that can be utilized to standardize:
- Storyboards: Share info about projects to educate and motivate. Pictures, graphs of key performance indicators (KPIs), useful tools, etc.
- Checklists: Facilitate adherence to standards
- Maps: Share processes, procedures, etc.
- Signboards: Vital info displayed at the point of use.
- Color indicators show correct location, items types, amount or direction of workflow.
- Alarms: A strong sign or signal when defined parameters are exceeded.

The Fifth S – Sustain
Definition: Outlines how to maintain and audit standards to ensure you don't slide back to old ways of performing. In other words, hold the gains!

Criteria:
- STICK TO THE RULES!
- To maintain discipline, practice and repeat until it becomes a way of life.

Benefits:
- Everyone in the organization knows what is expected of them.
- Correct and adhered to procedures become a habit.
- The workplace is well-ordered.
- Employee morale is higher.
- There is a cleaner, safer work environment and concern for the well-being of team members.

Why this will work:
- All employees are properly trained.
- Employees are involved and adapt the process for their work areas.
- Managers are deeply committed to implementing and maintaining the 5S's.
- It makes the job easier and less frustrating
- It makes the work environment look better, brighter, and more professional.
- *Large Visual Controls – with pictures, numbers and colors are critical to hold the gains.*

Reminder:
One top management member should tour an area once/week and provide verbal positive

reinforcement (the desired state) and recognition to employees through such means as personal thank you notes and open-ended questioning.

In Chula Vista, CA, 5S was used to address the finance library, front counter and personal workspaces:

Benefits:
- Improved communication within the department due to easy access to final documents
- Faster turnaround times in responding to the public
- Cost savings due to reduced orders for office supplies
- Avoided misinformation being released by getting rid of drafts
- Clear labeling to enable all employees to easily find materials, such as forms

Example of Chula Vista 5S approach and some of their wins:
- Eliminated out-of-date and unused forms that were cluttering the work areas
- More efficiently arranged fax and cash register areas for easier access and reduced traffic
- Developed visual management system for supply re-ordering
- Developed visual management and grouping system for forms
- Developed a good evaluation form to ensure sustainability (Figure 6.10)

6S EVALUATION FORM

6S Evaluation Form	Sort	Straighten	Shine	Safety	Standardize	Sustain
Level 5 Habit	Needed items can be retrieved in 30 seconds or less. Obsolete materials are routinely removed from the area. Preventative measures are in place to keep unnecessary items, reports etc. from entering the area. (1.0/25/75/50)	Anyone can walk into the work area and easily locate work by priority. Corrective measures are in place to address abnormal conditions. (1.0/25/75/50)	Work area housekeeping is a routine way of life. Corrective action measures are in place to address cleanliness issues. (1.0/25/75/50)	Workplace safety is a top priority and work teams routinely practice proper safety protocols. Preventative measures are in place to reduce/eliminate workplace injuries. (1.0/25/75/50)	Work team is adhering to standard work methods, visual and work area controls. A system of improving work methods and work area controls is clearly being utilized. (1.0/25/75/50)	Information on the area information board is meaningful and influences the daily decisions of the work area. Root causes of problems are eliminated and actions focus on preventative methods. (1.0/25/75/50)
Level 4 Commitment	All work material has been sorted according to what will be worked today, this week and this month. All other materials has been discarded or stored in central files. Materials, files and reports are routinely reviewed for necessity. (1.0/25/75/50)	Team members can easily determine what items are currently in-use and their priority. Visual controls are in place to indicate normal / abnormal work conditions. (1.0/25/75/50)	Work area housekeeping responsibilities are established and being followed as scheduled. Cleaning materials are stored and readily available. (1.0/25/75/50)	Regular meetings with staff regarding safety issues are held. Safety worksheet is posted and regular safety/ergonomic audits are held throughout Department. (1.0/25/75/50)	Team is utilizing standard work methods and work area controls on a daily basis. Does the team have good filing practices? Does the team have easy to follow rules guiding responsibilities? (1.0/25/75/50)	Work team routinely checks area to maintain the 6S's. Information on the area information board is meaningful to the work area. Source and frequency of problems are documented and corrective actions taken. Planning occurs to reach new 6S levels. (1.0/25/75/50)
Level 3 Organization Understanding	Only documents and tools necessary to the work area are stored at the work area and are stored in an orderly manner. (1.0/25/75/50)	A system has been established to highlight the order in which jobs will be performed. Visual controls identify elements of the work area. Is information understood about ledger and file reduction? (1.0/25/75/50)	Cleanliness problems have been identified and preventative measures are taking place. Visual controls and indicators have been established. (1.0/25/75/50)	Safety issues have been identified and preventative measures are in place. Ergonomic changes have been implemented and safety issues are discussed with staff (1.0/25/75/50)	Work team has documented needed items, work methods, visual and work area controls, and has made them available in the work area. (1.0/25/75/50)	6S presentation has been made to all Team members and a general understanding for the need and direction exists. Area information board is present, visible, and maintained. Do individuals know when work is completed? (1.0/25/75/50)
Level 2 Awareness of Need	Needed and unneeded items have been identified and unneeded items have been removed from the area. Nothing is placed on top of machines, cabinets, printers and computers. (1.0/25/75/50)	Needed items have been organized according to use including work procedures. Incoming and outgoing areas, including computer directories, are clearly designated and utilized. (1.0/25/75/50)	Initial cleaning has been performed. All office equipment is clean. Desks and cabinets are free of unnecessary objects. (1.0/25/75/50)	Safety worksheet has been completed. Basic ergonomic issues addressed (1.0/25/75/50)	Team has agreed on needed items, work methods, and work area controls. Hard for visitors to tell what type of work is performed and where, but employees generally know. (1.0/25/75/50)	Organization and employees have knowledge of and are employing some aspects of 6S. Have you begun creating methods that prevent backsliding? (1.0/25/75/50)
Level 1 Initial Effort	Needed and unneeded items have been identified. (1.0/25/75/50)	Items are neatly placed in the work place. (1.0/25/75/50)	Area cleaning is performed on a random basis. (1.0/25/75/50)	Workplace is generally clear of hazardous materials. (1.0/25/75/50)	Work methods have been developed. (1.0/25/75/50)	Some 6S awareness exists. (1.0/25/75/50)
Overall Score (Sum of Totals divided by 6) ___ /6 =	Total =	Total =	Total =	Total =	Total =	Total =

Figure 6.10

The Sixth S – Safety

Definition: Ensure that all safety policies and procedures are followed. Weight and location of items must be taken into consideration to minimize the potential for accidents. Ergonomics are also important when designing work areas (see Figure 6.11).

Final 5S (6S) Guidelines/Reminders

- Ensure "before" pictures are taken – this documents the progress that has been made.
- Develop "Elevator Speeches" for each 5S event (What are we doing? Why are we doing it? What can I do to help? and What's in it for me (WIIFM)?)
  - Communicate with ALL stakeholders about any 5S event beforehand
- Display prominently:
  - 5S charts in all key areas and in management offices.

1S – SORT

- Sort to a logical sequence:
  - Frequency of use – the more often used, the closer to the user
  - Safety – heaviest materials in the position for greatest safety consideration
- Remember Red Tag disposition criteria:
  - Ensure all members of an area understand the red tag concept and that everyone needs to participate to decide on disposition.
  - Ensure everyone knows what to do with Red Tag items – salvage, trash, re-cycle, auction, or...?

2S – STRAIGHTEN – SET IN ORDER

- Clearly label shelves, units, etc. initially with masking tape and clear bold lettering – ask others in the area to review and modify locations to make the most sense. Use PowerPoint paper signs to start with. Once locations are finalized, lock in with more permanent marking. Pictures, numbers and colors should dominate.
- Use a Home Depot or Supermarket approach to aisles, floor maps, laminated locator sheets, etc.

3S – SHINE

- Clean the area daily – everyone challenged to pick up in their area.
- Assign responsibility for clean-up – sign off list, daily, post prominently.

4S – STANDARDIZE

- Pictures posted on how areas should look – with numbers and colors.

5S – SUSTAIN

- One Top Management member to randomly tour an area once/week – kudos, Atta boys, open ended questioning (no yes or no answers), etc.

- Use deviations from standards as "learning moments" and not belittling employees. How do we prevent something from happening again?

6S - SAFETY
- Audit work areas to ensure safety policies and procedures are in place and being adhered to.

5S When It Comes To Computer Files And Email:
- Use a more detailed, richer description in the email subject matter area.
- Do not use the inbox as a storage file as it makes it harder to find emails.
- Create a simple "processed" folder to hold emails that you have read that you do not want to delete (or store in file system).
- Act on emails so that you really don't need them anymore.

Back to the rest of the 8 wastes:

3. MOTION: Any people movement that doesn't add value to the service or product. Areas of motion waste can include:

- How the work is laid out in the individual's work area, the general team work area and the department work area
- Spaghetti mapping and 5S to determine motion waste. Is there too much searching for items you need to do your job?
- Does the area allow for the best flow to get the work done?
- Are the ergonomics set up to minimize potential injury? An example from the Mayo clinic (Figure 6.11):

Motion Economy & Ergonomics*

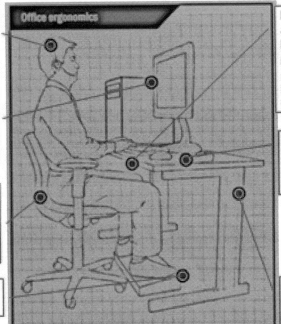

If you frequently use the phone, get a head set rather than cradling the phone on your neck

Place monitor directly ahead, about arms length away. Top of screen at or below eye level. Place monitor so that brightest light source to so the side.

Get a chair that supports spinal curves. Adjust height so feet rest flat on floor or foot rest and thighs are parallel to floor.

Get a footrest if your chair or desk is too high.

Place mouse in easy reach & same surface as keyboard. While typing, keep wrists straight, upper arms close to body, and hands at or slightly below level of elbows

Keep key objects (phone, stapler, etc.) close to body to prevent excessive stretching.

Desk should be high enough for clearance for knees (or lower chair).

*Source: Mayo Clinic

Figure 6.11

4. WAITING: Our experience working with Government processes is that waiting is the dominant waste category for time, in some cases exceeding 95% of the overall process time. Causes of waiting can include:

- Employees are absent on vacation, jury duty, travel or sick. There is no parallel process backup for the person, so the work waits until they come back to work. If the person is out, the status of their pending work, availability of their work instructions, etc., is unclear or unknown.
- The more process steps with more people involved and more handoffs, the more waiting. Drive to what we call "one- stop shopping". The ideal state for any customer is to do their complete transaction with one person or via a simplified website.
- Adding more time to any process generally results in less responsiveness and more required follow ups (waste). People should respond while it is fresh in their mind.

Another example of unnecessary waiting was an agency that held hearings with businesses that had violated statutes. The adjudicator had 90 days from the time of the hearing to file the judgment. The question was asked – why can't the judgment be rendered right at the hearing? In more 90% of the cases it was clear what the judgment was and delaying 90 days caused extra work, not to mention statute violations could continue.

- Certain work processes are only done on certain days of the week or weeks of the month. The best approach is to handle the request on the same day it is made and understand what process changes need to take place in order to make that happen.
- Work is accumulated and done in larger batch sizes, as other different types of work batches build. Later, we'll cover the need to minimize batch processing and move as close as possible to single-piece flow with balanced value added work.
- Too many unproductive meetings, including late starts, lack of meeting agendas, preparation, focus, lack of discipline. Many times, the main culprit of late starts is the meeting leader. Meetings should start on time and the minutes cover who was there and who was late. This isn't about figure pointing; it is about meeting the agreed upon standards of the meeting.
- Accountability for meeting time commitments is lacking. Just as commitments are made to customers to meet certain dates, the same should pertain to personally agreed commitments we make to each other. The responsibility standard that should be in place:
  - Commitment dates must be mutually agreed upon. These are never forced on someone or assigned to them in their absence.
  - Meet the date you committed to, or contact the person who the commitment was made to beforehand to let them know there is an issue and work out a new date or work to shuffle priorities if the original date is sacrosanct.
- Key equipment is broken down or being used by someone else. Understand if there are any bottleneck equipment issues and develop plans to remove these issues.
- Email responses take too long or require wasteful follow ups. The subject matter box in the email should be richer in content, which will drive quicker response rates. This means instead of saying "Info" in the title, the title should be more descript like "John I need the information on the closing by May 1". This also pertains to the "to" and the "cc" addresses on the email.

Too many approvals or reviews take place. A city's complete hiring process was just over 68 days from the submittal of the initial requisition to the new hire start date. In the process were three steps where that needed City Manager-Assistant City Manager approval. When the process flow and data were reviewed with them, two of these "reviews" were eliminated, resulting in a savings of almost 20 days. One approval time was 10.5 days – 3.8 days to submit and 6.7 days to approve. These extra steps had grown over time. Often approval steps result from a "problem" that happens and, rather than address the root cause of the problem and institute a permanent corrective action, another step gets added to the process.

- Too many signatures required. Signatures are tied to approvals. The question becomes, if there are eight signatures required instead of three, which process will be scrutinized more? The answer is that, with fewer signatures, the people involved with the process will take more time to check before signing. The more signatures, the more "I can't really look at this and someone else will review and catch any issues."

In one instance, a city auditor wanted to go to a local professional evening meeting that cost $50 to attend (the city would reimburse); it took five signatures for approval but how much did that really cost? There is also a level of difficulty in reducing the number of signatures related to "my level of importance" and "I don't want to be eliminated." "What if something goes through that I would have caught?" There are obviously areas involving financial transactions that should have a check and balance in place due to the potential for fraud, but are five checks and balances really necessary?

- Waiting for customers to submit or reply.
- Computer software or hardware changes or issues.

5. OVER PRODUCING: This is based on making too much and doing more than what is required to meet the stated goal, challenge or customer need. Some of the areas of overproducing:

- Too many unnecessary reports. This waste can result from a request that is made by a city council member to produce information for the next council meeting. This report gets added to the list and never subtracted. The preparation package for the meeting gets larger and larger. A periodic survey of report recipients is useful to determine what they truly need and use. When this is done, many wasteful reports or information can be eliminated.
- Duplications and redundancies – multiple data entries in separate systems. Many Government legacy IT systems are going through detailed reviews to update and eliminate overlaps.
- Inventory is a result of over producing, including storage areas.
- Doing things that are comfortable as opposed to what is needed.
- Lack of good work instructions and communication leading to process steps that don't need to be done.

6. OVER PROCESSING: Performing process steps that add no value to the product or service.

- Repetition in different forms. Too many forms or letters being sent out too frequently.
- Multiple approvals or signatures.
- Over-analysis or double checking.
- Duplication of efforts within and between departments and agencies. Unknown parallel efforts doing the same work.
- Too many emails and lack of email protocols. We have seen some Government managers receive more than 1,000 emails a day. Why is this happening? Can they possibly read everything? We encountered a manager with more than 5,400 unopened emails in his "in" box. Were important actions or information missed?
- New managers add more process requirements without reviewing what's already in place and eliminating process steps.

7. DEFECTS – This includes rework activities. When we work with Government, one of the first questions we ask is "How are you doing?" The answer we usually get is "We don't know" or some form of generality (good, great, fine), with no data available to support the answer. We have found that the area of defects (errors) and rework is largely unknown. As an example, we have seen a process with a one-page customer-submitted form with error rates across multiple regional offices of 77%! If it isn't right, then rework kicks in. Enormous amounts of employee time are attributable to these wastes. Some examples:

- The layout of forms or work makes defects likely. Forms are filled out incorrectly or incompletely. Information is missing.
- Inconsistent data stored in multiple software systems.
- Poor employee training along with a lack of standard work instructions.
- Doing things over or throwing things away.
- Misunderstanding the customer need.
- Difficult instructions for customers to understand.
- Customer addresses are wrong. One of the most popular processes we've worked with agencies to improve is undeliverable mail. In one case the savings were over $500,000. Mailings get sent out, the address files are not current and materials are returned, leading to rework and delays. Could this have some impact on why states have millions and sometimes billions of dollars in unclaimed taxpayer assets on their books?
- Communications are poor, leading to misunderstandings. For example; "Make sure you bring proof of birth." When a driver's license is produced the answer is "We need to see a copy of your birth certificate," which should have been what was asked for in the first place.

The guiding goal we should strive for is "Right the First Time". The questions to ask:
- How do we get this form, input, etc. right the first time?
- What are the obstacles to getting it right the first time?
- What steps can we take to error proof the process so we do get it right the first time?
- How can checklists be used to get it right the first time? Achieving this goal will eliminate rework. The thrust must be "how can we do this" and not "we can't do this because..."

8. UNDER-UTILIZED PEOPLE – This is the greatest waste of all. Employees work in the process and see what is happening. They have frustrations and, when they bring them to their supervisor's attention they can be pushed away with comments like: "I don't have time to help you," "We have to do it that way," and "Just do your job The organization is not utilizing or is underutilizing its human resource talent. Knowledge, skills, ideas and abilities are not solicited or, when given, are ignored. Employees know what is wrong or where the problems are, which can have significant financial impact if they are allowed to be proactive.

Misguided suggestion systems are often introduced to receive employee ideas. We view these as rejection systems for the following reasons:

- The employee submits an idea on a form – hands it to their supervisor, puts it in a suggestion box, sends it by email, etc. At that point the ownership for moving the suggestion forward is transferred to the supervisor to explore and develop.
- The supervisor is not as close to the area to know what the idea is all about and doesn't have the time to really work on the idea, so the idea languishes.
- The idea may go to a review team, whose members know even less about the idea, leaving it to get lost in the bureaucratic jungle.
- The employee keeps asking what's going on with her/his idea and gets frustrated with the answers or lack of answers. This then becomes "Why should I bother suggesting ideas when nobody does anything about it!" Or, later on, "See, I told them about this and nothing happened." Outcomes are employee disengagement and morale issues.
- Without a robust, active suggestion system (there aren't that many), the suggestion box becomes vacant.

Very successful idea systems are based on the employee taking ownership, developing the rationale for the idea, getting inputs from fellow employees, trying it out, and implementing it with supervisor concurrence. This will be explored further in the chapter on Kaizen – Dynamic Idea Generation (DIG) starting on page 169. Harvesting employee ideas is part of daily Kaizen. Small, frequent employee improvements over time accumulate to deliver a large impact.

Some other reasons for under-utilized employee waste are:

- Employee skills or talents are unknown or underused.
- The organization culture doesn't treat people with dignity and respect (high dignity and respect for all employees is a fundamental for a Lean culture).
- Supervisors have not been trained on how to work with and treat employees.
- Employees lack proper training.
- Management has no time to go to the work area (Gemba) to see.
- Poor leadership and/or "ego issues" pervade the workplace.
- Management doesn't acknowledge employees; there is a lack of recognition and instances of not listening.

CHAPTER SUMMARY - ELIMINATING WASTE: Lean Government is grounded in the ability for all employees to have a clear understanding for identifying and removing the eight wastes.

A survey in ASQ's Government Division, spring, 2017, newsletter cited the following categories of waste (Figure 6.12) identified by teams doing projects (this is how often this form of waste was present in their project):

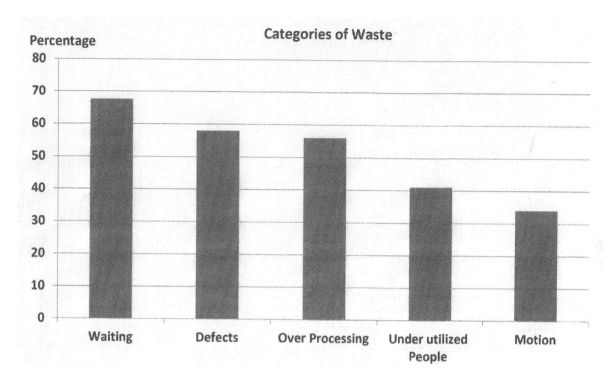

Figure 6.12

REFERENCE MATERIALS FOR FURTHER READING ON WASTE:

Tapping, Don and Gilreath, Michael (2017). *The New and Improved Lean Office Pocket Guide (2017) - Tools for the Elimination of Waste in ALL Types of Office Workflow Environments!*

Chapter 7
Problem Solving

"You got a problem, I got a solution."

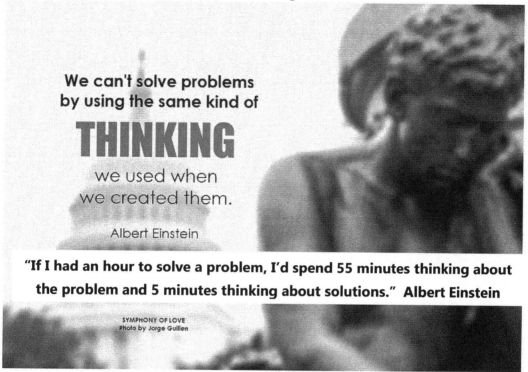

We can't solve problems by using the same kind of **THINKING** we used when we created them.

Albert Einstein

"If I had an hour to solve a problem, I'd spend 55 minutes thinking about the problem and 5 minutes thinking about solutions." Albert Einstein

SYMPHONY OF LOVE
Photo by Jorge Guillen

Problems should be seen as GOLDEN OPPORTUNITIES

We need to move from an environment where employees are afraid to surface problems to an environment where the surfacing of problems is encouraged and positively recognized.

If someone is asked are there any problems and the answer is "no," then that is the problem. People are afraid to point out problems. What about the current culture?

- Are employees afraid to bring up problems based on how they will be treated by their supervisor?
- Are identifying problems critical to organizational transparency?
- How do we encourage the identification of problems?

This chapter focuses on utilizing problem-solving for:

1. Solving specific current problems that will create immediate benefits.
2. Using a problem-solving process approach to move from the current state condition towards meeting a challenge goal/improvement target.

Great Lean Government organizations have widespread problem-solving proficiency throughout all organizational levels. This chapter will cover the reasons for having:

- Good operational definitions
- Good measurement systems
- Good data for generating clues to determine root causes
- Good problem-solving processes

OPERATIONAL DEFINITIONS

An operational definition is a precise description that tells how to get a value for the characteristic you are trying to measure. It is used to remove ambiguity, create a common understanding, and as a communication and reference tool. It also tells you what and how to measure.

- What: must have specific and concrete criteria
- How: must have a method to measure criteria
- Why: Must be useful to both you and the customer

The importance of operational definitions is to ensure everyone involved has the same understanding of what is being discussed.

For example, if someone said that they had to go to the Emergency Room (ER) at the hospital and it took two and a half hours, do you know when that time started and stopped without specifics? Did the time start when they got injured, left their home to go to the hospital, arrived in the parking lot, checked in at the admissions desk, or some other event? The same goes for the end time: was it when they got discharged from the ER, got in their car, drove to get their medications, got home, or another event?

So, this simple example of the ER experience highlights the need to be specific about what is being measured for everyone to have the same understanding. Some examples from Kaizen events, where the operational definitions were agreed to be:

- Procurement process time: Process Start – when Purchasing receives the agreed upon specification. Process Stop – when the PO is issued.
- Hiring process time: Process Start – when HR receives an approved requisition. Process Stop – the new hire's first day on the job.
- Public Works work order process time: Process Start – when the work order is entered into the computer at the service center. Process Stop – when the work order is closed out in the computer at the service center.
- "Right the first time" for a Work Order: The ability to do the work order as requested without additional information or research (it's rework to get more information = waste).

Operational definitions are used to eliminate subjectivity and interpretation.

An operational definition can be:

- a written statement
- a display of examples for comparison (e.g., color card)
- constantly-repeated group practice that forms the basis of consistent judgment

An operational definition should be:

- something people can really understand
- something that enables different people to reach the same correct conclusion
- something that enables the same person to reach the same correct conclusion at different times

Everyone needs to have the same understanding and know what we are trying to improve. Next, we need to ensure there is a good measurement system.

MEASUREMENT SYSTEMS

Cursory attention in the Lean literature (and many times no mention) is paid to ensuring there is a good measurement system in place before solving "the problem". More than 85% of the time, the measurement system isn't capable and needs to be fixed before proceeding further with a root cause analysis of the problem. What if the real problem is caused by a faulty measurement system and we don't know it? Some of the important measurement concepts include:

- **Accuracy**: Do the results match the actual value or expert assessment?

- **Repeatability**: Do we get the same results when making the same measurement more than once? For example, if a person takes three random measurements over time on the same process element, do they get the same results?

- **Reproducibility**: Do we get the same results when someone else completes the same measurement?

- **Stability**: Do we obtain the same measurement when repeated at a later time? We need to know if we have a stable process that's not fluctuating over time.

Why is this important? An example would be the Medicaid assessment process. Most states have more than 500 social workers doing Medicaid assessments. Let's say a social worker interviews a client at his/her home to make an assessment on what type of needs the client has and the level of support required.   One of the functions is an Adult Daily Living (ADL) skill called eating. *The operational definition of eating is: The ability of the client to take in food or liquids. This includes the ability to chew and swallow foods or fluids without reminder, physical assistance, prompting, or adaptive devices.* So how does the social worker measure this client capability? If the answer is a "yes" or "no" whether the client can eat on their own, then the data is totally discrete (similar to "on" or "off"). Does the social worker politely ask and get an answer? Do they ask to see the client demonstrate and get physical evidence (which may be somewhat awkward and embarrassing)? Or is there another means? This assessment ("measurement") then becomes the basis for the recommended client support or assistance. The opportunity for variation in this process is enormous with corresponding cost variability. For example, going from Meals on Wheels for five days a week to full- time assisted living support means a difference of more than $1,000 per week for one client! This has a huge cost consequence to Government!

The question then becomes: how 500 social workers assess or measure with a level of consistency? This now requires that the world of subjectivity is turned into a consistent measurement system. To get beyond "yes" or "no" assessment judgments, the best approach is to create training case scenarios with different personal capability levels (say a minimum of four, preferably six) and ask social workers to review the case scenario and assign a "1" to "4" value to it. Coupled with this would be the "expert answer" to the case scenario that the agency agreed was correct. What we want to know:

Repeatability: would one social worker get the case scenario right each time (three times presented the same scenario randomly)?

Reproducibility: would three social workers each get the same case scenario right each time with randomly presented case scenarios?

It is practical, however, to test a case worker against the expert value. If they don't pass, then the root cause has to be determined and it's usually more about training and having well-documented guidelines or standard work (with pictures, colors and numbers) to make the various assessments. This testing must be established on a frequency level to ensure stability over time. For example, an annual qualification or certification could be given.

Moving forward to solve a problem without verifying that a good measurement system is in place is a recipe for disaster.

DYNAMIC DATA COLLECTION TECHNIQUES
Solid Data Collection is the basis for Solid Problem Solving

The foundations for improvement are data and facts. The expression "In God we trust, everyone else please bring data" reflects that good decisions are based on data, not opinions. Yet, many solutions are based on opinions.

The power of simple data collection:

1. See what is happening, which generates clues for

2. What corrective actions can be taken to solve the problem and

3. Move the expectation for "right the first time" as close to the initial source as possible.

These data collection techniques are called "dynamic" because they can be used in the actual work area (the "Gemba") on a daily basis to capture simple data using pen or pencil and a paper checklist or image. They also provide clues as to the true causes of things like problems, errors or rework.

This minimizes the need to have what you might call "organized guesswork" tools such as brainstorming, affinity diagrams, and fishbone diagrams. These techniques are intended to capture as many ideas as possible and then combine and rank them based on a group consensus of which ideas have the greatest leverage. An example of a more graphical representation of the accumulated root causes is called a fishbone diagram (or Ishikawa diagram – Figure 7.1). This is an example of the variation in how far a catapult propels a golf ball:

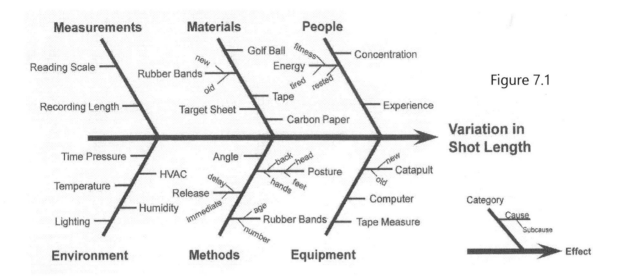

Figure 7.1

The reason we call these approaches "organized guesswork" is that they are based on mostly opinions and they generate many possible causes that may contribute to the problem (assuming everyone has the same understanding of what the real problem is). Then there must be a means of ranking the possible ideas (or countermeasures) to try. If the countermeasure creates the desired results, it's a solution.

The positives to brainstorming, affinity diagrams and fishbone diagrams:
- A cross-sectional group is involved and different perspectives come forward.
- All ideas are encouraged and no ideas are criticized.
- Others can build and expand on an idea that's presented.

The negatives to these approaches:
- A subject matter expert's ideas can be ignored or combined into a broader category when the subject matter expert really does have a good countermeasure to try and group dynamics overrule.
- Most everything is based on opinions and not hard data or facts.
- The problem to be solved is not clarified and understood by the team before generating countermeasures to try.

We have found that *the process is far smarter than the people* who are trying to solve the problem. The best approach is to go to where the problem exists to best understand what is happening in the process and develop a means of collecting useful data. This will be covered more in the chapters on Process Mapping and Kaizen events.

One of the first questions to ask is "how are we doing?" In the case of Government, many times the answer is "we don't know."   This is also usually followed by a lack of knowledge or understanding of what the customer truly needs or wants. If we don't know how we are doing, then we don't have a starting point to know how we're going to improve and how much we did improve. It's like driving with no speedometer.

So, we look at a process to develop some data. The data generates clues as to the areas that are generating the problem root causes. We want to use simple techniques that can easily capture data, take very little time and can be applied directly at the work area by the employees who perform the day-to-day job. This rarely involves an IT or computer solution, at this stage. The dominant techniques are check sheets, frequency plots and concentration diagrams, as explained below.

CHECK SHEETS

These are simple grids that list job activities that are done, frequencies that they happen, or times they consume, rework and rejects, and other items that may be appropriate to the process. Check sheets standardize both the data that is collected and the data collection process.

An example of processing forms in a work area:

Action	>1 min	1-3 min	3-5 min	5-8 min	8-12 min	12+ min	Rejects	Rework
Form A	IIII	II	III	卌 卌 II	II	IIII	I	
Form B	III	IIII	I	I			IIII	II
Form C		I	卌 III	卌 卌 III	卌 卌 卌 卌 III	卌 卌 卌 卌 卌 卌 I	III	卌
Form D		III	IIII	I	I		I	1

Figure 7.2

A simple check sheet (Figure 7.2) was developed for how long it takes to complete each form and the number of times this happens in the course of several days. Rejects (errors) and rework are also on the check sheet. Collecting data is a simple matter of making a tick mark on the sheet with a pen or pencil. We can see that Form C clearly dominates in frequency and, more importantly, the amount of time dedicated to processing this form. We can now focus our attention on Form C to better understand and determine root causes of why the processing takes so long and then develop an improvement strategy. Reducing the time on form C has huge leverage in the overall process.

Remember: Run a trial check sheet early on to make sure it's accomplishing its intent.

Other examples could include:
- Amount and type of phone calls the city/agency is receiving
- Amount and type of complaints the city/agency is receiving
- What forms have errors when the public fills them out

FREQUENCY PLOTS

A frequency plot is used for collecting continuous data. It creates a picture that graphically displays important characteristics about the process variation.
- Use a frequency plot check sheet with continuous data such as:
  - Types of undeliverable mail
  - Types of phone calls received
  - Time required to respond to a customer request
  - Amount of time to process an application

An example of a frequency plot in a state DMV agency looking at Interstate trucking renewal applications (Figure 7.3):

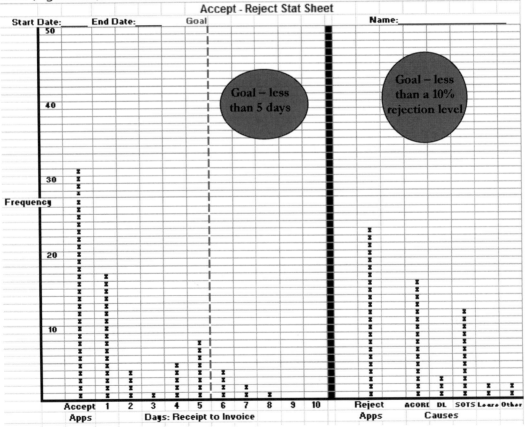

Figure 7.3

This was plotted daily by each employee in the unit. Prior to using this form for data collection, the agency didn't really know how it was doing or where to find the biggest issues impacting agency performance. The left side of the frequency plot shows how many days from the receipt of the application to the invoice being sent out, including how many applications were accepted (far left side). The goal is to be less than five days, when the previous experience was an average of 18 days (which was unknown when the project started). On the right side of the plot is the amount of rejected applications, along with the frequency of causes. It's very easy for the supervisor to take this data from the employees in the work area and compile the data each week to issue the performance report for the unit.

This unit was able to go from five to three people through attrition (one retired) and the other person was promoted into another area, along with reducing the receipt to invoice time from 18 days to two! The rejected applications went from 45% to under 9% within three months! Excellent employee engagement and the data visibility led to improvement ideas. As always, the approach to productivity improvements with Lean should be handled through creating greater capacity to do more value added work. *Reductions in staff should be only done via attrition, not layoffs. If Lean results in improvements with a need for less people and they are laid off instead of redeployed, then the enthusiasm for Lean drops.*

CONCENTRATION DIAGRAMS

A concentration diagram is a data collection form used to record data directly on a picture, form or chart.
- It's a graphic representation of the item being measured.
- The visual pattern is never random, there are always areas that dominate the data (hence, "concentration").
- It can show where and the type of defects or rework occurs.
- It graphically illustrates patterns and clusters.
- Lengthy verbal descriptions are not required.
- It's a quick and easy way to collect meaningful data.
- It requires a physical product or picture/form.
- It can become cluttered if there are many types of defects, rework, or occurrences.

Concentration diagrams are used to detect contrasts in problem areas. They create huge leverage for making improvements when looking at the data accumulated on the diagram. A concentration diagram can monitor the location of a defect or problem with respect to a process, form, or area in order to find associated non-random patterns. Non-random patterns yield clues about the nature of the problem. Concentration diagrams can be utilized in any work areas, including police crime analysis, fire incidents, accidents, potholes, garbage, complaints, rejected applications, and computer form errors.

A case study in Boca Raton was undertaken to understand the level of accounts payable errors and root causes (Figure 7.4) and then develop countermeasures to try. A simple check sheet concentration diagram was developed and data was captured over a short period of time by the employees working in the process. Department names were protected so no one would feel like blame was directed toward them. Remember, another tenet of Lean is that most everyone wants to do a good job. The data results:

Accounts Payable Error Tracking: Period: 03/17-03/28							
Type of Error	Dept 1	Dept 2	Dept 3	Dept 4	Dept 5	Dept 6	Total
Invoice was sent to the Department 1st instead of AP		1	55	4	5		65
Receiver was not entered timely	5	1	6	25	5		42
Missing, wrong or invalid PO #		1	20	8	2	10	41
Receiver amount or qty incorrect			5		8		13
Receiver duplicated			7				7
No invoice					1		1
Total	5	3	93	37	21	10	169

Figure 7.4

Looking at the data, we now have concentrated areas where errors were happening. Working with Department 3 would focus on 55% of the errors (93 of 169) while "invoices sent to the wrong department first, instead of AP" was in excess of 38% (65 of 169). This makes it much easier to come up with countermeasures that can be tried, since we know which areas cause the greatest impact.

If we take the frequency plot example from the previous interstate trucking application renewal process and now look at the highest cause of errors, which were the Acord insurance forms (Figure 7.5), we see the following:

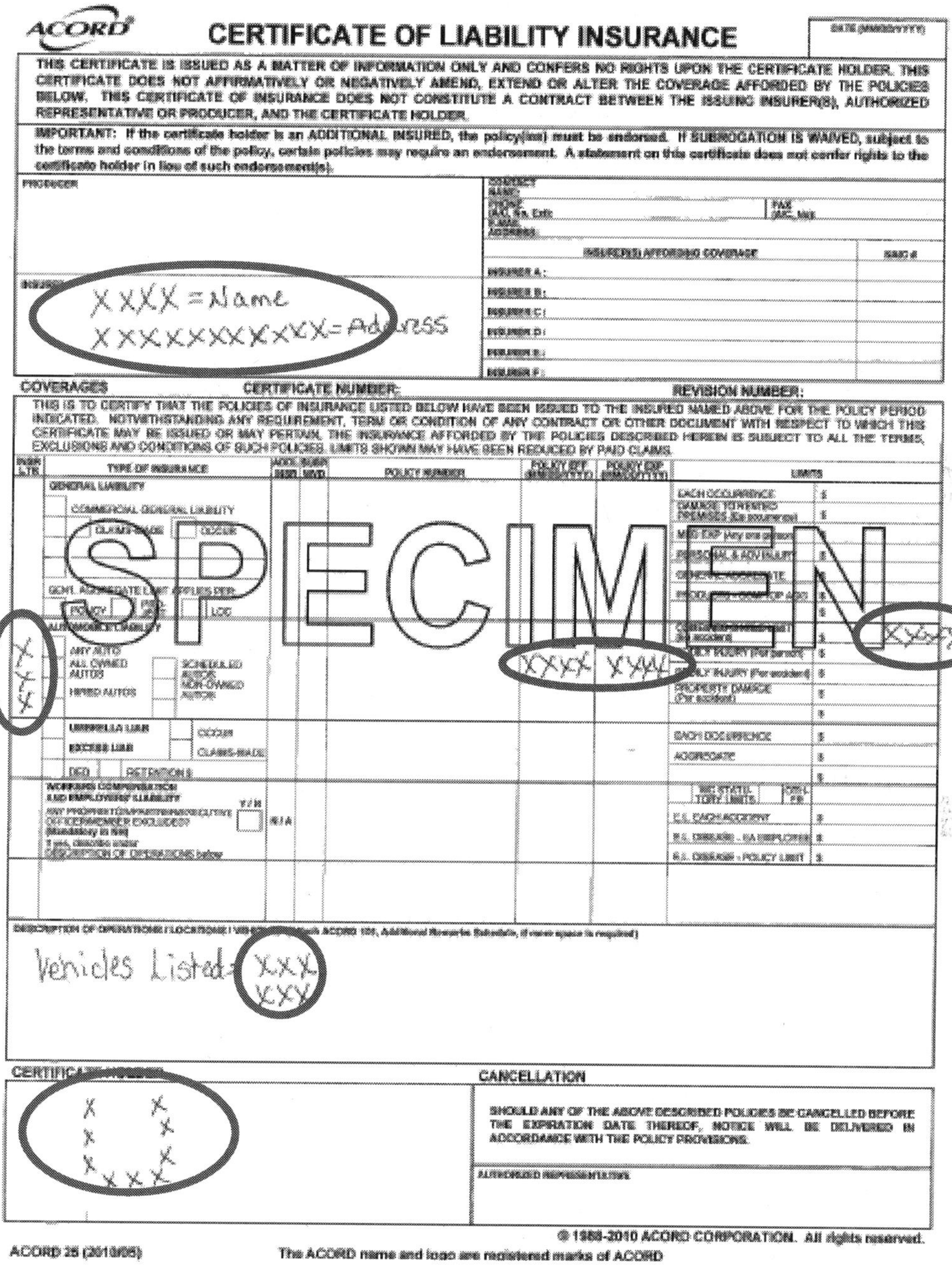

Figure 7.5

The circled areas show the concentration of errors on this insurance form. Having this information facilitates:

- Working with the insurance companies to better clarify the information that's coming through incorrectly.
- Working with the trucking association to help them be more proactive with the truckers and insurance companies to ensure forms are filled out correctly.

- Working with the various trucking companies on what information needs to be correct.
- Modifying the internet site and written instructions to address how to fill out the forms, prioritizing where the most errors occur.

Another example was in a city public works department that was experiencing high accident and worker's compensation rates. Concentration diagrams were used in a 24" by 36" color display near the time clock where all employees could see their safety performance (Figure 7.6).

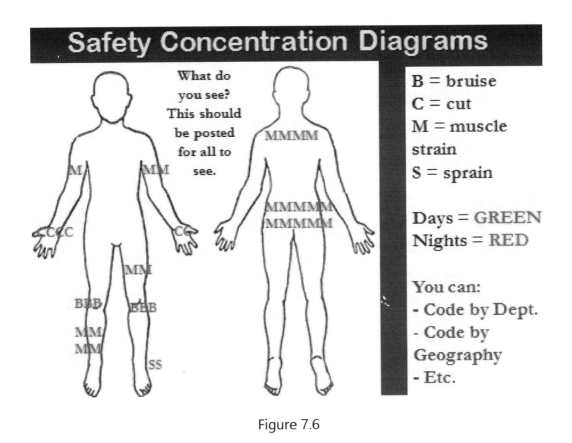

Figure 7.6

Seeing the actual safety results by cause and by shift caused all employees to be more aware of the safety issues and root causes when they were at work. Obviously, back muscle strains were the #1 candidate and the discovered cause was that the City purchasing department had gone from 25 pound bags of salt for the wintertime to 50 pound bags of salt for winter sidewalk operations, causing more back injuries.

Concentration diagrams are very powerful for looking at:
- City crime data, by type, by location, by time of day for more effective police patrol deployment

- Fire data by location, type of fire age of population, and time of day, which led to a more aggressive fire prevention program along with more outreach to the elderly
- Any forms that are in use as to where errors or rework is occurring
- Computer data entry errors, which can be captured by printing screen images and then marked where the concentrations are leading to screen consolidation or redesign, indicating where more training is needed for affected employees

Summary benefits of daily data collection in the work area include:
- It's a very visual representation of the process issues.
- It fosters high employee engagement and idea generation as to causes and potential solutions.
- Data drives changes in work instruction content and sequencing.
- Daily data can easily be rolled up to weekly or monthly data for a broader or more long-term picture.

Once good operational definitions, a good measurement system and good data collection techniques are established, the work can begin on problem solving.

PROBLEM SOLVING

PARETO CHARTS

The Pareto chart was developed in the 1500s by an Italian economist named Vilfredo Pareto as he studied the distribution of wealth in Italy. He concluded that 80% or more of the wealth was in the hands of 20% or less of the population, hence the "80-20" concept evolved, popularized by Dr. Joseph Juran. The Pareto chart creates visibility as to where improvement focus or problem solving should be done to create the greatest impact or leverage. It's the well-known concept of where to "get the best bang for the buck."

An example of a Pareto chart is shown below, in Figure 7.7:

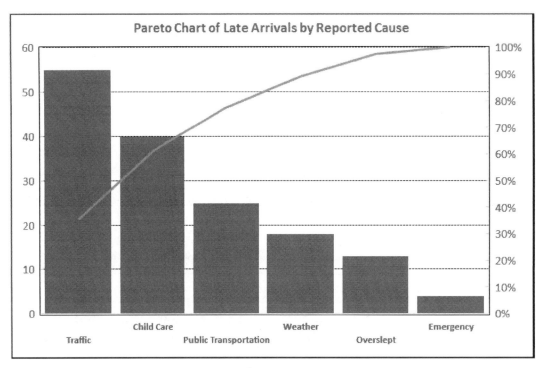

Figure 7.7

The bar on the left is the area with the highest frequency, with subsequent data in descending order to the right. The last bar on the right could be another specific cause or "other," which would be the sum of the remaining data causes. The line on the chart is the cumulative sum of each of the bars to make up 100% of the data. So, Pareto charts direct us to where effort should be focused. In some cases, multiple Pareto charts may be used as one could show frequency of causes, while another could show cost or savings impact of each cause. It's a matter of selecting what area provides the greatest impact or leverage for making improvements.

FIVE WHYS

When children are young, parents always dread getting into a discussion when the child would keep asking "why," sometimes incessantly. Normally, asking "why?" results in a defensive "because" response and can be coupled with a level of irritation. From a Lean perspective, asking "why?" five times is like peeling back an onion to get to the true root cause. It can't be seen as a personal inquisition or attack. The focus is on what happened in the process to cause an unexpected outcome. It may take less than five whys, or it may take more; however five is a rule of thumb. It might be a single path of inquiry, or multiple five why paths may emerge.

Five whys is the simplest root cause analysis tool. Once again, it should be utilized in concert with data or facts, when possible.

- The goal is to get past surface level causes to root causes.

- Keep asking "why" to each "cause" offered until the underlying root cause is found and a countermeasure can be tested.

An example of using 5 Whys (Figure 7.8):

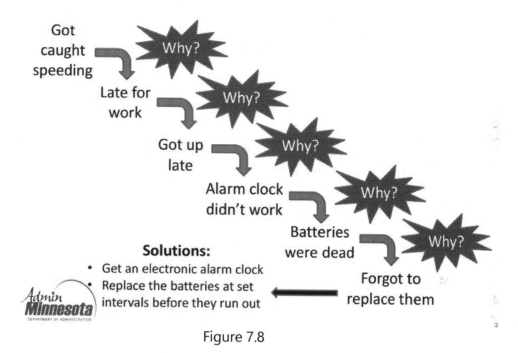

Figure 7.8

PDCA or PDSA[1]

Plan-Do-Check-Act (PDCA) is a method for scientific problem solving. It's also the main means for moving from the current state toward a goal or future state condition. For example, let's say we need to reduce our new business licensing time from 38 days to five. There needs to be a methodology to break down and solve the problem, and PDCA dominates in Lean. Dr. Deming viewed this as Plan-Do-Study-Act (PDSA) and Toyota adopted and adapted it to become Plan-Do-Check-Act. For the purposes of this book, PDCA will be used. An illustration of PDCA is shown in Figure 7.9 below.

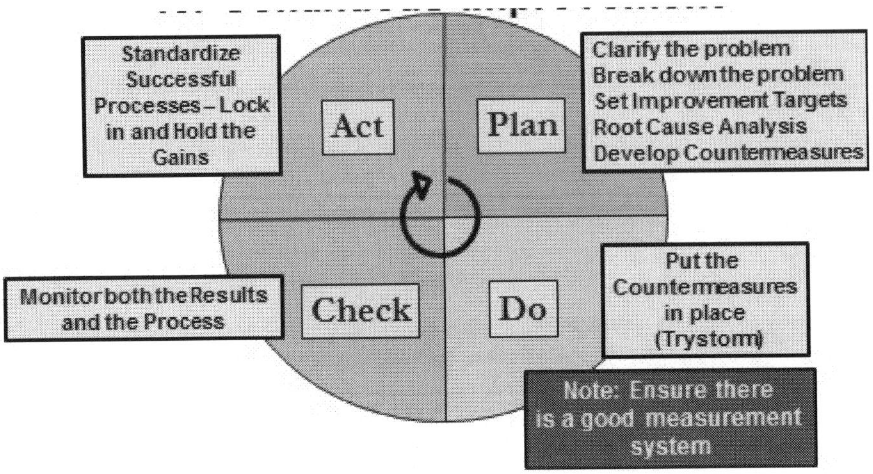

Figure 7.9

As stated by Albert Einstein in the beginning of this chapter, determining what is the real problem is the most critical part of PDCA.

P = PLAN – this stage involves the first five steps in the overall PDCA process:

1. Clarify the Problem

This is the most important step. If you're in a meeting and someone says, "I have this problem", how often is time spent truly identifying the definition of that problem or do the participants just dive in with assumed causes or solutions?

As an example, look at how to improve education in K-12 schools. Everyone thinks they are experts because they all went through the system. Ways to improve the educational system range from more money for education, better teacher evaluation criteria, improved student testing outcomes, better pre-school programs, and the list goes on.

So, clarifying the problem is paramount. After having a good operational definition, a well-written problem statement should contain four major elements:

a. A description of the concern, problem or opportunity. The problem described should be a known, verifiable, or measurable fact, not a guess or an assumption.

b. Background on when and where the problem happens or is observed.

c. One or more measures indicating the magnitude or extent of the problem.

d. A description of the impact, consequences or threat presented by the problem.

In other words, what is the pain associated with this problem?

2. Break down the problem into more detail and identify gaps

Are we guessing what the problem is or do we know?

What clues do we have as to potential root causes?

What data do we have?

Brainstorming, fishbone diagrams, affinity diagrams are last resorts; if no solid process simple data collection is available.

Are there good operational definitions for consistency?

Is there a good measurement system? This is another critical area and virtually all the Lean literature doesn't adequately consider the impact of a good measurement system. If the measurement system is bad, a tremendous amount of effort could be expended on working on the problem, when fixing the measurement system would make the problem go away.

> **Make sure there is a good measurement system in place that's measuring the correct process parameters before proceeding.**

3. Set improvement targets

Determine what is a good first improvement step, based on the facts or data.

These first targets form the basis of determining some trials ("trystorming").

4. Analyze the underlying causes

Data from the actual process is the key to generating clues, rather than guessing. Go and see the actual process.

Where does the real problem occur?

- Binary search? Does the problem occur in the first half of the process or the second half? Continue to split the process in half to take a deeper dive.
- Pareto analysis?
- Simple data collection? Checklists, frequency plots and concentration diagrams provide solid clues.

5. Develop Countermeasures

- Based on the first four steps, what do you want to do for your first experiment?
- A countermeasure is a *potential solution* that needs to be tried and proven out.
- This sequence will need to be recorded on a PDCA cycles record (an A3 could also be used, as explained later).

Tools that can be utilized in the Plan phase include:
- Project Charter
- Elevator Speech
- Stakeholder Analysis
- Simple Dynamic Data Collection techniques

- SIPOC chart (Supplier-Input-Process-Output-Customer)
- Swim Lane Mapping
- Benchmarking (see Chapter 5 on Benchmarking).

D = DO

6. Trystorm the Countermeasures
We now try countermeasures that we think have a good chance of being effective in solving the problem or moving us toward the goal.

Tools that can be utilized in the Do phase include:
- Dynamic Data Collection
- Direct observation
- PDCA cycles record

C = CHECK

7. Now we see what happened – did we achieve the desired results?
This is the review of the Do phase. Were the results we expected achieved or not? Was the countermeasure we tried effective? The results of Check take us to the Act phase.

Tools that can be utilized in the Check phase include:
- Dynamic Data Collection
- Direct observation
- Specific metrics
- PDCA cycles record

A = ACT

8. Lock in the gains, or go through another PDCA cycle.
If the results weren't what we expected or wanted, then we do another PDCA cycle with a new countermeasure. If we achieved the desired results, we now must ensure that these gains are sustained through visual controls and standard work (Figure 7.10). Are we satisfied with our result and the progress we made? If so, we move on to another problem or challenge to work on. If we still have good leverage to make more improvements in the same original area, then we would do another PDCA cycle to improve again.

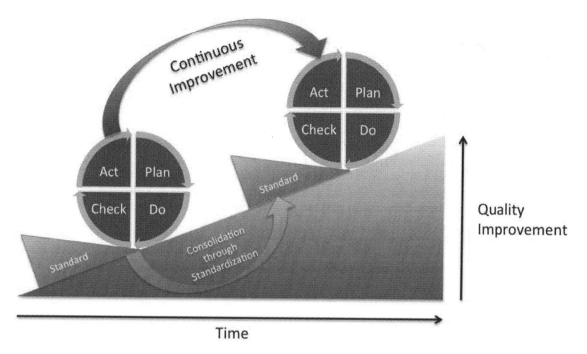

Figure 7.10

Tools that can be utilized in the Act phase include
- Visual Controls (covered in Chapter 9 – Standard Work)
- 5S (covered in Chapter 6 – Eliminating Waste)
- Standard Work (TWI, or Training Within Industry – Chapter 9)
- Follow up intervals at an agreed to frequency, with a specific process owner assigned

A client example utilizing PDCA to visually track improvement ideas in a work group (Figure 7.11). They are tracking the ideas as they progress through the PDCA phases.

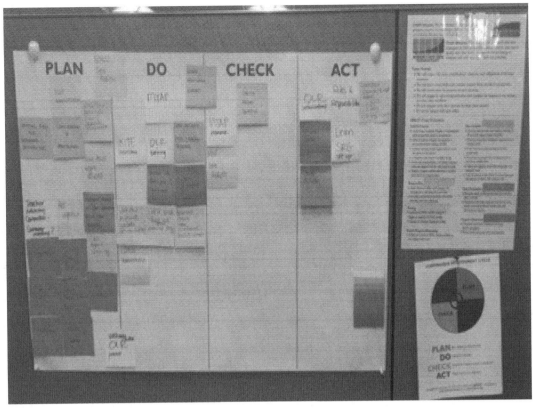

Figure 7.11

A3

A3 is an excellent tool to use to characterize the steps of thinking through the process of how to attack and document a key project or problem. The name is derived from the ability to put the storyboard of a project on an A3 sheet of paper (about the size of American 11" x 17" paper).

An A3 can be used for:
- A proposal or project charter
- A storyboard – to cover what was accomplished and to post for sharing
- A problem-solving tool based on the Plan-Do-Check-Act cycle

There are numerous format varieties for A3s. This format will be used for illustrative purposes, as shown in Figure 7.12:

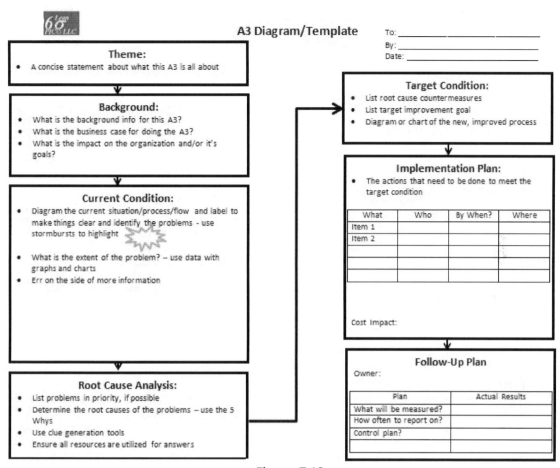

Figure 7.12

Theme = a concise statement that states the summary of what this project is all about. The theme is similar to the problem statement on a project charter (Chapter 10), but usually with a narrower scope.

Background = info, business case, organization impact and/or its goals. The business case could be the same as what is used in a project charter, just more condensed.

Current Condition = diagram or map the current situation and the extent of the problem using data or graphs. Use starbursts to highlight problems or issues.
Now we're looking at the real problem and what data supports this.

> *Overlooked in virtually all A3 training materials –ensure there is a good measurement system (Reproducibility & Repeatability). Most times the measurement system is not good. If the work hasn't been done to verify a good measurement system is in place, wasteful work can be done solving the problem when the real problem could be a faulty measurement system.*

Root Cause Analysis = list the problems (priority order); determine root causes (five whys, dynamic data collection, etc.). The emphasis on root cause analysis must be on what the data tells us.

- Go for facts, not opinions.
- The key is to use clue generation to focus in on the true root causes. Utilize the Dynamic Data Collection tools: Pareto Diagrams, Check Sheets, Frequency Plots and Concentration Diagrams (Note: Brainstorming, Affinity Diagrams, and Fishbone Diagrams are subordinate to real data/clue generation).
- This is done in the Gemba (actual workplace), not in a conference room or office.

Target Condition = list root cause countermeasures, improvement goal, diagram or chart the new process. Countermeasures (experiments) are tried to address the identified root causes.

Implementation Plan = what needs to be done to meet the target condition - who is doing what by when and where? Included here should also be the projected cost impact.

- This part of the A3 establishes who, will do what, by when.
- It's based on one owner for each step of the plan.
- Accountability and responsibility is clear for executing the plan.

Follow Up Plan:

- What will be measured and how often?
- What is the control plan to hold the gains and not slip backwards?
- What is integrated into the upgraded Standard Work?

PROBLEM SOLVING SUMMARY: Everyone in an organization should understand how to identify and solve problems. The rational sequence is: establish good operational definitions; ensure there is a good measurement system; collect real process data at the work site (avoid brainstorming, affinity diagrams and fishbone diagrams in an office or conference room); and then dive into root cause analysis and problem solving to meet the challenge goal.

Developing proficiency in problem solving takes practice and coaching. PDCA can be utilized to solve nagging problems and also as a methodolgy to move from the current state toward meeting a new challenge/goal.   If everyone becomes a problem solver, then employee engagement, accountabilty and responsibility, along with morale, make huge strides forward. In a Lean Management System, problem solving at all levels, is part of the culture.

REFERENCES:

[1] Moen, Ronald D. and Norman, Clifford L. *Circling Back – cleaning up myths about the Deming cycle and seeing how it keeps evolving,* Quality Progress, http://www.apiweb.org/circling-back.pdf

REFERENCE MATERIALS FOR FURTHER READING:

Liker, Jeffrey K. (2009). *Problem Solving the Toyota Way,* McGraw-Hill Professional.
Shook, John (2008). *Managing to Learn: Using the A3 Management Process*, Lean Enterprise Institute.

Chapter 8
Process Mapping – Learning to See & Value Streams

"When you come to a fork in the road, take it." Yogi Berra

"Learning to See"[1] is the overarching concept in process mapping. When we talk to Government managers, we always ask if they ever take the time to truly observe the details of a critical process and talk to the involved employees. We rarely encounter anyone who does. They're just too busy and don't know how to "see". During Lean Government introductory two-day boot camps, we encourage attendees to take at least a half day (hopefully a full day) within 10 days of the boot camp completion and pretend they're on vacation and then immerse themselves in a key process that's causing "pain". Though this happens less often than we would like, the attendees who do this exercise tell us what an eye opening experience they had. They never realized processes were so messed up, training wasn't good, and what forms and procedural steps that were eliminated were still in place.

We worked with a city police department that had five chiefs over the last seven years. The current chief had come up the chain of command over a period of 22 years and felt "everything we are doing is value added." He didn't know. Meeting with small teams of officers on the beat, they were frustrated by the required amount of paperwork which was taking them away from community policing. Too much time was "desk work". A review of everything they had to do revealed some forms and paperwork from each of the previous four chiefs were still in place and were required to be completed. No one had ever had the time to review the process to determine what should have been eliminated. Furthermore, the paperwork they did came into headquarters, where there was even more work compiling reports and data filing – much of this could have been eliminated. No one understood or took the time to "see". As in this instance, processes grow and morph over time into more waste. The capacity to provide greater service is sidetracked. Even more employees may be requested when, in essence they aren't needed.

This chapter will cover various process mapping techniques: Process Flow Charts (not the first choice yet this is what most organizations use), SIPOC maps, Value Stream Mapping, Swim Lane Mapping, and Spaghetti Mapping. *It's imperative that any form of process mapping originates through direct process observations and the capture of detailed information with each step of the process.*

What is a process? A process is a sequence starting with an initial input and proceeding through a series of steps involving resources to generate the desired output for a customer. In manufacturing, the process could start with suppliers providing materials to be transformed into a finished product. In Government, many processes start with the customer providing the initial input to obtain the desired output (for example, obtaining a driver's license). It's imperative to ensure processes have the capacity to meet demand.

PROCESS FLOW CHARTS

These are the most familiar process mapping techniques, since this is what people have learned or been told to use.

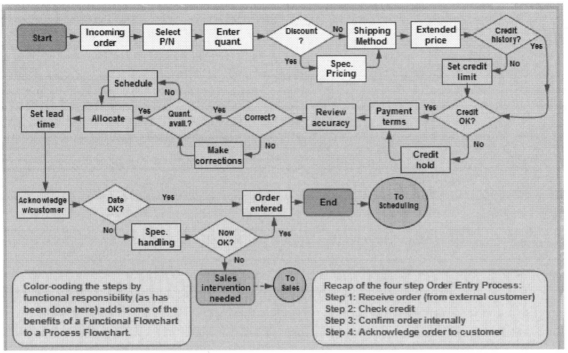

Figure 8.1   Source: Resource Engineering

The example in Figure 8.1 follows the flow of the process from start to finish. The most popular symbols used are:

What information are we lacking in Figure 8.1? Was the process map done based on direct observations of the process, or in a conference room or someone's office? If it's not a replication of direct observation of the process, then the validity of the map is seriously called into question.

Assuming all the steps were captured through direct process observation, what information is unknown or missing? What is the time between each step? How long does each step take and how much time is waste vs. value added? How many people work in each process step? What is the amount of work queued up (inventory) between each process step? What forms, computer screens, documents, instructions are used in each step? What are the defect/error and rework percentages at each step? What ideas and frustrations do the employees have to improve the process? What is the time required in the process to keep pace with customer demand (Takt time – more on this later in this chapter)? And the list could go on. The main point is that most process flow charts have many deficiencies and are never a good basis for improving a process.

SIPOC (Supplier-Inputs-Process-Outputs-Customer)

A SIPOC map (Figure 8.2) is a high-level view of the key steps of an overall process. It's a process macro view and framework that is further developed as the project is developed. SIPOCs can be helpful when establishing an initial Project Charter (Chapter 10). When doing detailed process analysis work, a Value Stream Map (VSM) or Swim Lane Map is much more relevant to use.

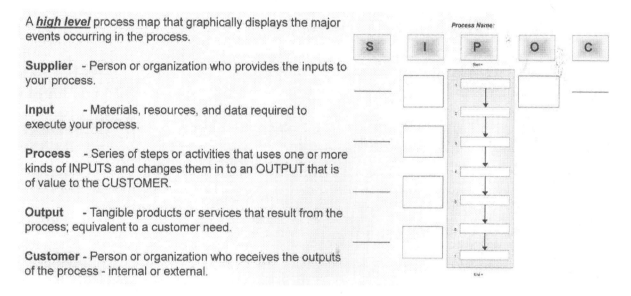

Figure 8.2

VALUE STREAM MAPPING (VSM)

A Value Stream Map (VSM) is a process flow mapping technique from the point of requested need to the completion of all activity and focuses on value. It can be very broad based in nature or have a narrower scope. This is the core approach to process mapping.

Here is the sequence that is followed (Figure 8.3):

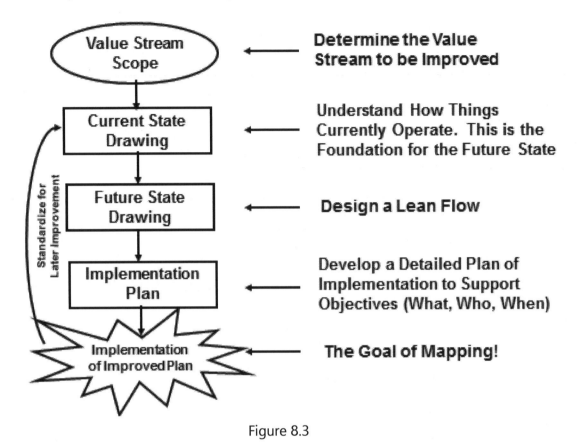

Figure 8.3

For example, Figure 8.4 illustrates a series of macro processes involving the King County, WA, Finance and Business Operations Division (FBOD):

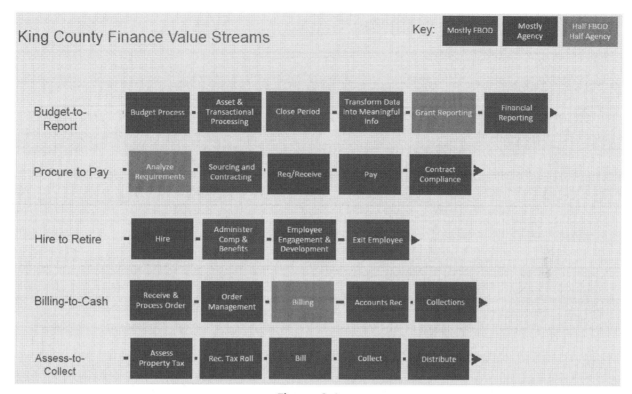

Figure 8.4

The major operations areas involve mostly FBOD, mostly another agency, or a combination of both (shared). Looking at the Procure to Pay Value Stream macro map, the Pay function could then be selected and creating a corresponding VSM for the Pay process.

Improvement Projects would then be prioritized based on the leverage of improving certain process steps in the Pay value stream based on the detailed VSM. The basics of Value Stream Mapping are as follows:

- Develop the Current State or As Is Map – defines the process as it currently exists. No work should be done on making any improvements until all the detail is captured from the current state analysis, observations and interviews.
- Develop the Future State or Proposed Map – shows the process as we would ideally like it to be once we have a solid Current State mapped out.
- Start with the customer in the upper right hand corner and the supplier(s) in the upper left hand corner. In the case of Government, many times the customer provides the input information (such as application for a business license) and receives the output (a business license).

A simple administrative process VSM Current state map:

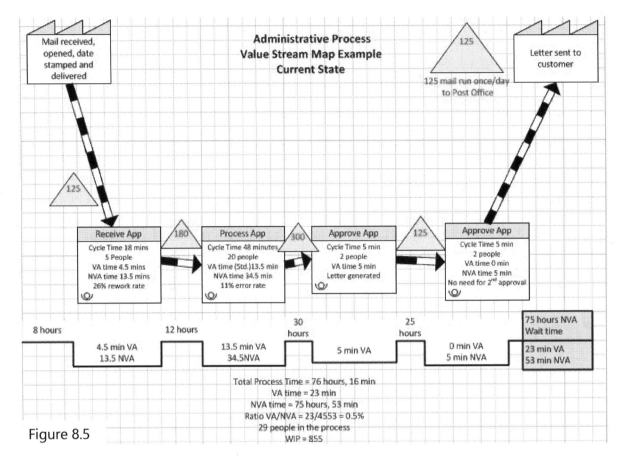

Figure 8.5

In Figure 8.5, there is much greater detail, such as:
- How much Work-In-Process (WIP = Inventory) is queued in front of each step
- The name of each process step, the overall work cycle time to complete one application, how many people work in the process step, how much of their time is Value-Added (VA) vs. Non-Value-Added (NVA), and rework or error rates. Distance traveled, forms, work instructions, computer screen copies, employee ideas and frustrations, etc. should also be captured.
- The timeline at the bottom tracks VA vs. NVA times, along with the rolled up summary information: VA time of 23 minutes, NVA time of 76 hours, 16 minutes; WIP of 855. The magnitude of the waste is enormous as the VA time is 0.5% of the total process time. There are also two approval steps, when only one was really necessary.

Once all of the information is captured in the Current State VSM, that information can be utilized to construct a Future State VSM map, eliminating as much waste as possible, which follows in Figure 8.6:

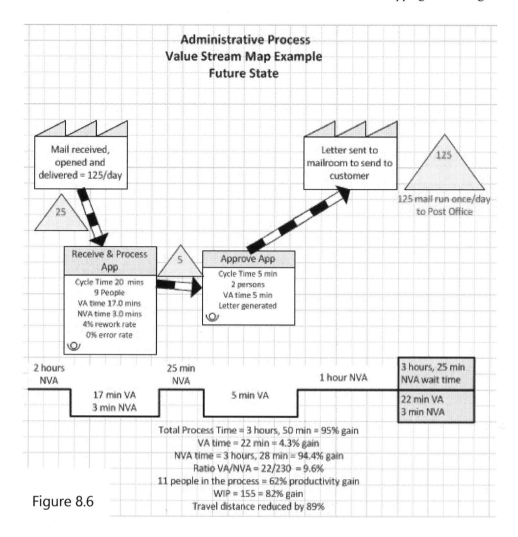

Figure 8.6

The gains from the Current State VSM to the Future State VSM yielded very significant results: 95% reduction in total process time, mainly based on the elimination of NVA time; productivity gain of 62%; WIP reduction of 82%: and travel distance reduced by 89% . Plus, even more time can be saved by receiving information electronically and sending the approved application electronically.

Some VSM symbols that are used:

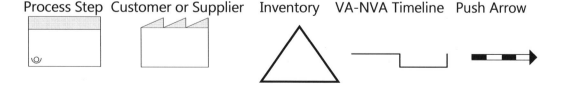

More VSM symbols are listed in the reference materials at the end of this chapter.

Figures 8.7 and 8.8 illustrate a form to collect process data and potential process interview questions to ask:

QPIC, LLC Value Stream Data Collection Sheet

Process Step/#:				Name:				# doing step:	
Previous Step:				Next Step:				Location:	
Work Sequence	Cycle Time	VA	NVA	Perf. Data?	Forms	Reports	Rework/Errors	Improvements/Ideas?	

Other Comments/Notes:

Figure 8.7

Possible questions to ask while "Learning to See"

What is done at this process step?

    What is the actual real work time?

    What adds value?

What is waste?

How is the layout?

Spaghetti Map the area?

    What can be eliminated?

    What can be combined?

    Distance between activities in this process step?

    When do you have to wait?

      For how long?

    What are your frustrations?

    What improvement ideas do you have?

    What can be improved immediately?

    What interruptions do you have?

    How many approvals are required?

    What needs to be stored and retrieved?

    Are there safety/ergonomics considerations?

    How much rework takes place?

    Why does the rework happen?

    How does it get addressed?

    How often?

    What happens if there is an error?

Why?

Why does the error happen?

How does it get addressed?

How often?

5S needs?

Standard work needed?

What would be the future/ideal state?

    Always keep the "5 Whys" in mind to

    get to the true root causes

What's the next step in the process?

    How and when does the handoff take place?

    Distance to next step?

    How long does something wait before

    it goes to the next step?

Measure What Matters:

    1. What do customers really care about?

    2. How do you know how you're doing?

    3. Are the metrics visibly posted?

    4. Metrics drive improvement opportunities.

      Analyze them for problems->root causes.

Figure 8.8

SWIM LANE MAPPING

Current State Mapping - Swim Lane Maps are, in our view, the process mapping approach of choice in Government for developing more detailed current state and future state maps (Figure 8.9).

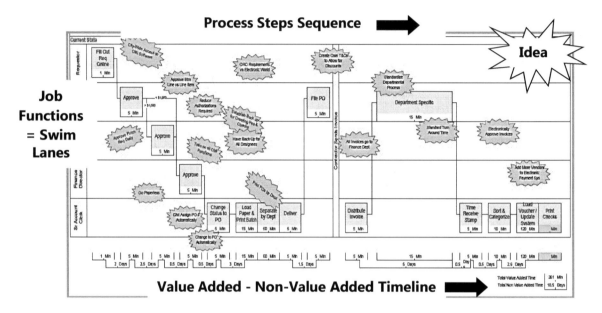

Figure 8.9

When it comes to Swim Lane Maps, it is important to:

- Establish the start and stop points of the process.
- List each of the major steps in the process.
    - Use the vertical axis to list each participant in the process. This could be an individual, department, location, etc., with each participant constituting a horizontal "lane". List the more detailed activities and decisions that make up the process.
    - Identify the order in which the steps occur, placing the steps in the lane of the participant that performs that step/activity/decision.
    - Arrows are used to connect the elements of the diagram and show the flow of work. Different arrows can be used for physical vs. electronic movement.
    - Be concise. Use as few words as possible for your labels.
    - Be inclusive. Involve the employees who work the process and include their multiple perspectives. Don't rely on just one employee.
    - Don't expect immediate consensus. There is richness in engaging different views of the flow.

- Map the process as-is -- not as you believe it is, want it to be, the SOPs say it is – but as it actually is.
- Confirm your map. Interview those who work in the process but weren't directly involved in the mapping. Observe the process in action, first hand.

The information that is gathered includes:
- Process performance data. The process step, who does it, and the time required, broken down to total time, Value Added [VA] time and Non Value Added [NVA] time. There may also be some Value Enabling time or steps. Distances between each process step impact the process flow and layout.
- Employee frustrations and improvement ideas
- Amount of time between each process step (wait times)
- Forms, reports and computer screens used -- get copies and computer screen print outs
- Defect and rework rates (real data)
- Work area Spaghetti Map
- If the process meets the customer demand rate
- The number of the 7(8) wastes that are in each process step
- Things that can be combined or eliminated
- Customers' needs and if they are being met
- Performance metrics posted in the area to know "how are we doing"
- Safety, health or environmental issues
- Work instructions that are numbers, colors and picture-based
- Good standard work that is audited for compliance by the supervisor

This list is not all-inclusive but it represents the need to capture the current state details of the process and represent it on the Swim Lane Map. Even with all this information, it is important to resist any attempt to immediately impose solutions.

Some Swim Lane basics:
- Assemble the process improvement team (cross-functional including members that work in the process, materials handlers, and some people who don't know much about the process).
- Do a quick walk through first – start at the end and work backward to get a flavor for the process.
- Then, physically go through the process in detail. Capture the information listed above that's relevant to the process under review.
- Have a stopwatch, if needed.
- Pencils, post-its, and large paper sheets (a roll of 36" wide paper works well) to put on the wall as the base for the map.
- Digital camera, DVD recorder (capture the "before"), and the process, if needed *.

*These are sensitive areas that employees should have a "heads up" about beforehand as to why they are being used. It isn't about "gotchas" or blaming people; it's all about improving the process.

Some Swim Lane mapping tips:

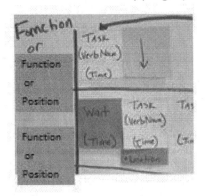

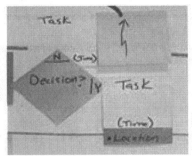

1. Every time you change lanes, there's a handoff
2. With every handoff, there is almost always a wait
3. Putting information into storage requires a task and file/store denoting the storage location
4. Every decision should have a task for "yes" and for "no"
5. Subsequent tasks appear to the right of the prior task, unless the task occurs simultaneously (e.g., meetings)

There are variations in approaches that are used with Swim Lane Maps, based on user preferences. In all cases, 3M is very happy with the amount of post it notes™ that are consumed!

Swim Lane Future State Mapping
Once the current state map is completed with all of the glorious details and information gathered, it is time to determine what the future state should look like.

Several key concepts need to be covered at this stage to complement all the information gathered from the current state:
1. One Stop Shopping.
2. Takt time – the pace of customer demand.
3. Balanced work flow and layout guidelines.

1. ONE STOP SHOPPING IS THE GOAL (THE IDEAL STATE)

Seek to do "One Stop Shopping" (Figure 8.10) whenever and wherever possible. Processes need to be designed and driven so the customer is able to transact business with only one person. Remember the Ontario, Canada, survey study earlier in this book. There were no handoffs, no delays, no waiting for someone else to respond – one stop! This is a fundamental principle that must be in the thoughts of everyone as processes are designed and/or improved. The focus must be on "how we make this process one stop shopping" and not "we can't do this because".

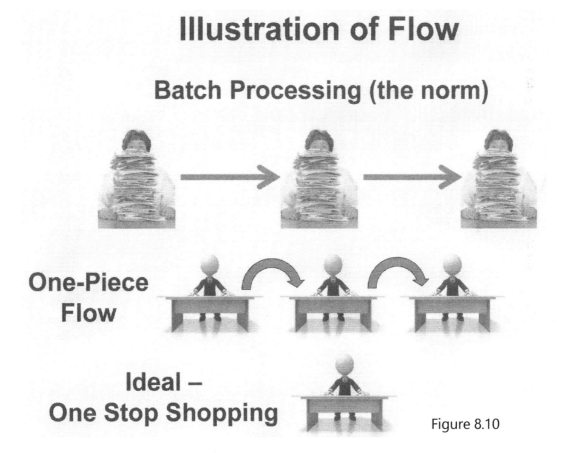

Figure 8.10

Running a simulation in boot camps, we find that batch processing a poor flow, current state process will yield a 1 on the numerical productivity scale for the simulation. One-piece flow will yield a 3-5 productivity level (300-500% better) and one-stop shopping will yield a 7-10 productivity level (700-1000% better). This all has to do with the minimization of waste. Of course, in real world situations, these productivity gains will be different. While most people feel that batch processing is the most efficient way to operate, the simulation drives home the counterintuitive point that single-piece balanced flow is much more productive.

Certainly, there are cases where job restrictions or union contracts may make job changes or consolidations difficult. This should not deter efforts to move to the one stop shopping approach, although it may take some redesign, negotiations and job re-evaluations.

The one main exception to this principle is when it comes to transactions involving money and the potential for fraud. In these cases no more than three people (ideally two) should be in the entire process chain.

One stop shopping drives super customer service, enhanced employee satisfaction due to broader job scope and flexibility, and lower overall costs. One stop shopping involves several key concepts:

Current state mapping analysis. This forms the basis for designing the future state process in the most value added and least wasteful way possible. This is a great start.

2. TAKT TIME – THE PACE OF CUSTOMER DEMAND

This is the maximum time required to keep pace with customer demand. Ideally, this should have been done during the current state analysis. It's a German phrase and we equate it to the "drumbeat" of the process. Remember Takt as the ninth person in the eight-man skull boat racing crew calling out the stroke pace (Figure 8.11):

Figure 8.11

To establish Takt time you need to know customer demand rate and available time to meet the customer demand. In a simple example, there are 100 people going to the DMV today for their car license plate registrations. There are three employees in the area and their available time is: 8-hour day (480 minutes) – less lunch, breaks, and a fatigue factor = 400 available minutes/person X 3 = 1200 total available minutes. Takt time would be 1200 minutes divided by 100 transactions = 12 minutes per transaction. This is fine to provide customer service if the average time to do the actual work is less than 12 minutes per transaction. What if the work takes 17 minutes? Do you add more full-time people, bring in temporary workers or work overtime? Before doing any of these "solutions" (you may have to respond short term with overtime or temps to keep pace) a solid review of the process needs to be done to look at process flow and VA vs. NVA steps to eliminate wastes; this usually pays big benefits and avoids excess costs. Takt time is a key to providing early warning signals of the potential to have customer service or process issues and take early corrective actions.

3. PROCESS FLOW AND LAYOUT

Drawing from another DMV example, there was a public area that handled car license transactions. The desired flow pattern in a Lean work sequence is a U pattern, where all steps in the process are within line of sight:

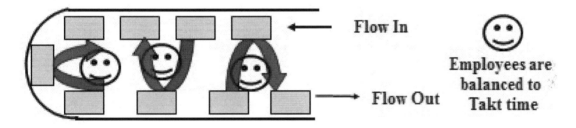

This pattern allows for maximized flow, communications and coordination. Of course, one stop shopping would only have one person doing the entire process sequence (always the goal).

SPAGHETTI MAPPING – MAPPING THE ACTUAL PROCESS FLOW

The Deputy Commissioner had heard about a U cell layout and laid out the public room at the DMV this way:

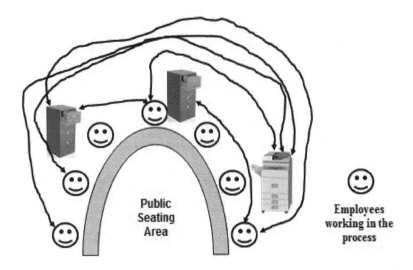

Only part of the process Spaghetti Map was drawn here. Each employee station could provide a license, but each employee had to travel to multiple areas to get the license, the paper files, copy materials, etc. The public sat in the middle, waiting to be called. The process motion and transportation waste was obvious.

Spaghetti mapping is one of the first mapping steps that's done to understand a "bird's eye view" of the process flow with associated motion and transportation wastes. The actual, to scale, process area is drawn on a map and then lines are drawn following the actual process sequence. The usual result of this mapping is that the process flow looks like a bowl of spaghetti.

Reversing the physical layout resulted in a much more efficient and less costly process. All employees were inside the U shape cell with easy access to everything they needed with far less motion and transportation waste:

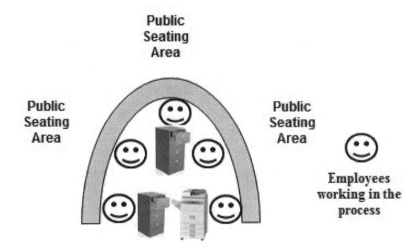

Figure 8.12 is another Standard Work map (spaghetti map) example of a process with the sequenced, numbered process steps and the distances traveled.

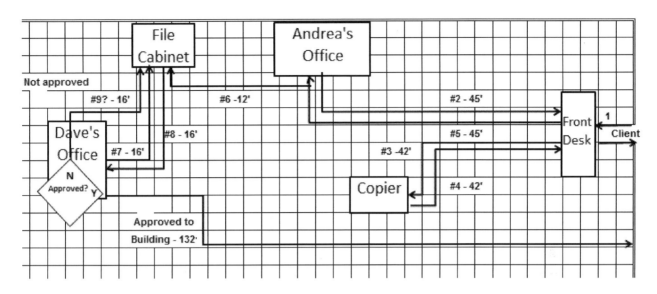

Figure 8.12

CHAPTER SUMMARY- PROCESS MAPPING: The key takeaway is to ensure that sufficient time is spent to truly understand all the process details of the current state before even thinking about implementing solutions to move to a more improved future state. Swim lane mapping is the best approach to use to capture all of the current state process detail leading to an improved future state map.

REFERENCES:

[1]Rother, Mike and Shook, John (April 2009, Version 1.3). *Learning to See*; Lean Enterprise Institute, Cambridge, MA.

REFERENCE MATERIALS FOR VALUE STREAMS AND PROCESS MAPPING:

Martin, Karen and Osterling, Mike (2014). *Value Stream Mapping: How to Visualize Work and Align Leadership for Organizational Transformation*; McGraw-Hill.

Chapter 9
Standard Work

How do we do things around here?

Standard Work (As the work is routinely, actually done and observed)

Standard Work refers to the standardization of the best current work practices. (This is not work standards; it is the standardization of the way we work.) It's a simple written description of the safest, highest quality and most efficient way known to perform a particular process or task. It's the only acceptable way to do the process (which reduces worker variation and improves consistency). It's the baseline for holding the gains and continuously improving to a better level of Standard Work.

Standard Work meets customer demand rate, includes the necessary process quality checks to minimize or remove defects and rework, and establishes the level of Work in Process (WIP) for each process step.

Its objective is to make process operations repeatable, ensuring consistently efficient production and reduced variability of output. This also allows for better, consistent training.

This is done by applying Standard Work techniques to document all aspects of current work practices, thereby providing the basis for improving the process. Standard Work should be applied to all work processes, including leader and management work.

The late Philip B. Crosby wrote the book *Quality is Free* in 1979. Phil's last job before starting his consulting firm in 1979 was Director of Quality at ITT Corporation, which at that time included the Sheraton Hotel chain. He was fond of telling this story (heard at one of Phil's seminars, paraphrased):

A Sheraton in New York City was having problems with customer complaints due to inconsistent quality in how the rooms were cleaned and made up by the housekeeping staff. Phil found that there was a high turnover rate and the housekeeping staff spoke in excess of 20 different languages, creating an impossible training situation, since they didn't have trainers on staff who could train in all the languages. Phil's approach was to have the staff make up the perfect room and bathroom. Then they took pictures and put numbers on the pictures on each page in the training manual in the sequence the work should be done. With pictures and numbers in a manual attached to each housekeeping cart, all the housekeeping staff could understand the sequence of how the work should be done and what the final finished room and bathroom should look like, no matter what language they spoke and understood. The complaints and quality issues evaporated.

This is a simple example of how Standard Work was put in place. The more that pictures, numbers and colors are utilized, the better the consistency of the work. Simple, visual instructions and training is best. Once Standard Work has been put in place, there must be an audit process in place as well to ensure the Standard Work is being adhered to and how to address corrective actions.

Standard Work:

- Focuses on experienced employees

- Comes from the work area – "Learn to See"

- Focuses on the elimination of waste

- Builds teamwork vs. individual incentive

- Provides the game plan and basis for training new employees in the work area

Standard Work involves several key concepts:

1. One Stop Shopping.

2. Takt time – the pace of customer demand.

3. Work in Process Inventory (WIP)

4. Process flow and layout and work sequence.

5. Balanced work levels.

6. How to create Standard Work.

7. Training Within Industry (TWI) work instructions.

1. ONE STOP SHOPPING IS THE GOAL (THE IDEAL STATE)

Seek to do "One Stop Shopping" whenever and wherever possible. This was covered in the future state process mapping discussion in Chapter 8 on Process Mapping.

2. TAKT TIME

This was also covered in the future state process mapping discussion in Chapter 8.

3. WORK IN PROCESS (WIP)

This is the minimum amount of inventory (work to be done) ahead of the particular process step in order for the process flow to be optimum to meet Standard Work. If there is too much, work may start to pile up and downstream delays may occur. If there is not enough, work may dry up and the process may have starts and stops.

4. PROCESS FLOW AND LAYOUT.

This was covered in the future state process mapping discussion in Chapter 8 on Process Mapping. In addition, the deadly 7(8) wastes need to be identified and eliminated. Identifying transportation waste through Spaghetti Maps is extremely useful for reviewing process flow.

Work Sequence

Work sequence is the order and timing of how an employee performs manual operations.

Work sequence determines the manual operations cycle time.

Work sequence differentiates between the manual and the machine processing sequence.

Focus remains on the manual work sequence.

When machines are involved in the process and, if they are the pacing operation for overall process time, they are known as "Monuments". It's like cooking a lobster by first preparing the whole work area with butter, plates, lobster forks, etc., while the lobster has yet to be put in the steamer. The lobster will take 8-10 minutes to cook no matter what is done, so engage that process step first (the steamer) and start cooking the lobster. The other steps for preparing the lobster meal are within the internal time the lobster is cooking. This is a simple example to illustrate the need to determine if the overall process cycle time has some machine (monument) constraints.

5. BALANCED WORK LEVELS

What to look for in the work area with manual work:

- **Waste.** The eight forms of waste.

- **Variation.** Large variations in processing time, quality, etc., impact flow. If not addressed, work must be adjusted to meet the slowest staff member.

- **Too much work**. If a staff member is overburdened (too much work, not enough experience for the job, or too much non-value added in the work), the load must be balanced. If this isn't done, the potential for defects and rework increases.

A **Producer Loading Chart** can be developed based on the times gathered from the various jobs in the work area. In the example below, there are -four different jobs in is this process. The Takt time has been determined to be 45 minutes and the workloads between the four employees is not balanced. The first logical step would be to shift and balance the work content between the employees so each would have 45 minutes of work and meet Takt time.

Before: Unbalanced Flow

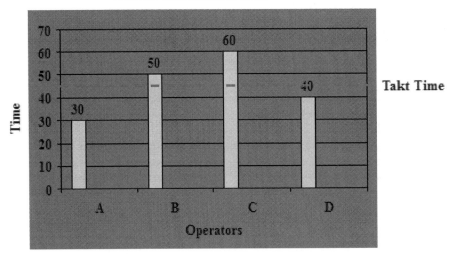

After: Balanced Flow

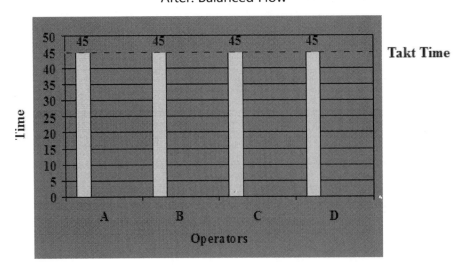

In either the unbalanced or balanced flow state, work needs to be done to determine the value added (VA) and non-value added (NVA) work and remove the NVA work. The resulting producer loading chart may then look like this:

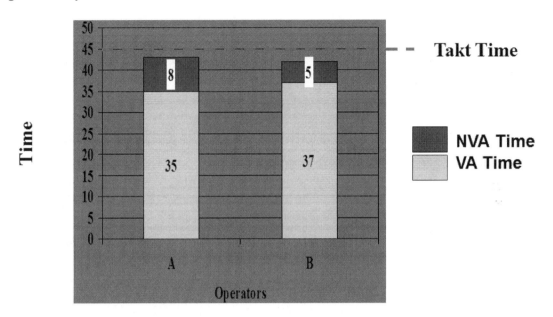

With a value added analysis of the jobs and the waste removed, we are able to do the work with two people, freeing up two people to be redeployed to other work to provide better service and more capacity.

6. HOW TO CREATE STANDARD WORK:

A. **Define the process for which you're developing Standard Work**. Where does the process start and end?
   - Standard Work must be developed for each step in a multi-step process.
   - Everyone who does the same job will use the same Standard Work (such as in the Crosby hotel housekeeping example).
   - The end point will be the starting point for the next Standard Work.

B. **Determine the Standard Work requirements.**
   - Name of the work process area
   - Takt time
   - Work flow area map and sequence
   - Who owns the process and who else needs to approve?
   - Location of the Standard Work in the work area

C. **Collect the necessary information:**
   - Identify the best practices and integrate them.

- Observe multiple people doing the same work. Everyone says, "I do it the same way" when, in reality, not many do it the same way. Standard Work reduces the person-to-person and site-to-site variation.

D. **Create Standard Work documents:**
  - Use visual instructions as much as possible, leveraging pictures, colors and numbers.

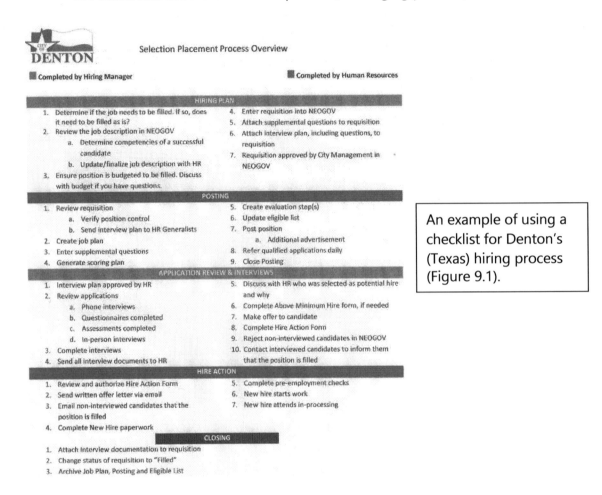

An example of using a checklist for Denton's (Texas) hiring process (Figure 9.1).

Training Within Industry (TWI):

This approach has become more prevalent in Standard Work documents. This was developed during World War II to meet the needs of the military. The actual TWI materials can be Googled on the Internet. Alan Robinson and Dean Schroeder wrote an excellent article on TWI in 1993[1] which provides the evolution and use of TWI. The foundational principles of TWI are in this TWI two-sided summary card (Figure 9.2):

HOW TO INSTRUCT

Step 1 – Prepare the Worker
Put the worker at ease.
State the job and find out what he/she
    already knows.
Get worker interested in learning the job.
Place in correct position.

Step 2 – Present the Operation
Tell, show and illustrate one IMPORTANT
    step at a time.
Stress each KEY POINT.
Instruct clearly, completely, and patiently,
    but no more than can be mastered.

Step 3 – Try Out Performance
Have worker do the job, correct errors.
Have worker explain each KEY POINT to
    you as he/she does the job again.
Make sure the worker understands.
CONTINUE until you know, he/she knows.

Step 4 – Follow Up
Put worker on their own. Designate to
    whom he/she goes for help.
Check frequently. Encourage questions.
Taper off extra coaching and close follow-
    ups.

*If Worker Hasn't Learned,
The Instructor Hasn't Taught.*

Figure 9.2: This is an example of a two-sided TWI card from Ceptara, Corp.

The TWI Standard Work form utilizes pictures, numbers and colors. The use of words are minimized. This format becomes part of a solid employee training process. Supervisory auditing to this format is also easy.

An example of a TWI document from a city Public Works department (Figure 9.3) follows. Compare this to a lengthy verbal training manual set of instructions on how to do the job.

Job Breakdown Sheet

Description of Task	BRUSH COLLECTION – DRIVER	
Tools and Supplies Required	CDL Driver's License, Brush Checklist	
Safety Equipment Required	Hard Hat, Safety Vest, Gloves, Safety Shoes, Earplugs, Safety Glasses	
Important Steps	Key Points	Visual Image
1. Before leaving the yard, walk around and inspect the truck and chipper attachment. Complete vehicle and chipper checklists.	Turn on vehicle and listen for any unusual sounds, vibrations. Make sure all lights, including headlights and brake lights are working. Inspect for any loose parts, leaking fluids, etc. Ensure all hitches and attachments are secure. This is to prevent any accident that may occur due to something being missed upon inspection. It will also prevent the loss of time having to return to the shop for repairs.	 
2. Drive brush route correctly.	Follow streets on brush list in order given. Reference map as necessary.	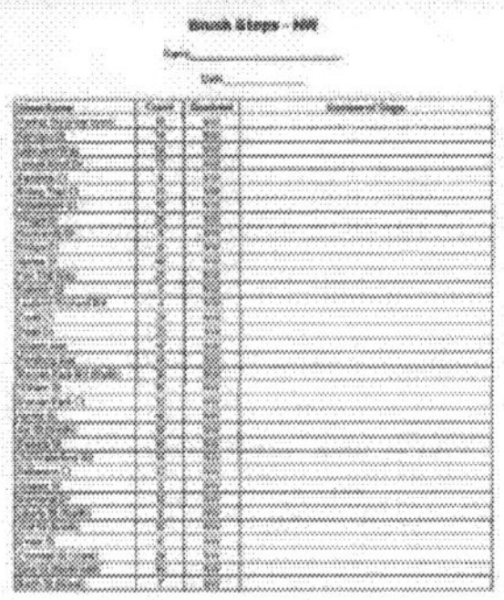
3. Stop at brush piles.	Stop at a close enough distance to avoid excess trips from pile to truck.	
4. Write down address.	Write address on checklist to confirm pickup has been completed.	*See Image from #2*

Figure 9.3 (Leesburg, VA)

E. **Train the supervisor on the Standard Work** – the supervisor is the owner. The supervisor must clearly understand the Standard Work and be able to train employees to do the work consistently, without variation.

F. **Audit the Standard Work for adherence and consistency**. This is an example of leader Standard Work (Figure 9.4):

Figure 9.4

There are a series of cards with specific Standard Work steps in a folder at the work site. The leader or another supervisor would randomly pick a card and observe the performance of the Standard Work. If it was done correctly, the card's green side is posted; if not, the red side of the card is posted. The purpose of doing this is to:

- Make it visible to everyone that Standard Work is being audited. Visual controls create sustainability.
- Have a metric for percentage compliance to visually display each week. People are challenged to increase the compliance metric.

- Determine the root causes for non-compliance and implement corrective actions. Once again, it's never about blaming people.

GEMBA WALKS

Walking the Gemba (Figure 9.5 - the area where the real work is done) to observe and talk to employees is another form of leader Standard Work to check adherence to Standard Work and also solicit employee improvement inputs.

Figure 9.5 – A Gemba walk at a metrics board.

TRANSFERRING/DEVELOPING EMPLOYEE OWNERSHIP (IN GENERAL):

1. **Train and explain expectations**. You'll never achieve ownership by telling, presenting and/or lecturing. Communications are always an area that can be enhanced but will not by itself create ownership. Utilizing an elevator speech should always be done when communicating changes:
   - What are we doing (the change)?
   - Why are we doing it?

- What do you expect out of me? The role the employee needs to play must be understood.
- What's in it for me (WIFFM)? A beneficial outcome needs to be shared. It makes the work easier and reduces levels of frustration, resulting in happier customers, which makes for a more satisfying day.

2. **Demonstrate, as necessary**. Being able to see the expected or desired outcome creates a greater level of understanding. Not only should the supervisor demonstrate, but the employee should also demonstrate that they understand or more training may be required.

3. **Employees should explain their understanding of what's expected.** The supervisor asks the employee to describe and show what needs to be done. Any employee questions or suggested improvements are helpful in making the process steps better.

4. **Commitment is important.** Asking the employee "will you do it" puts more ownership in play. If they can't say "yes," then the reasons need to be explored and corrective actions (such as more training) can take place.

5. **Employee sign-off is optional.** The employee signs off on the Standard Work instructions, which is a higher level of commitment and ownership.

6. **Audit to ensure compliance** (supervisor/managers). Leader Standard Work needs to review compliance with the employee Standard Work.

7. **Address "issues" the "Lean Way."** Treat everyone with dignity and respect.

8. **If Standard Work is willingly not followed, then disciplinary action is the absolute last step.**

G. **Make the necessary adjustments to the Standard Work if they are warranted based on actual experience and hold the gains each step of the way.** Evaluate the result (in a PDCA cycle). Continue to improve the Standard Work (Figure 9.6) until other Standard Work areas have greater leverage for making improvements.

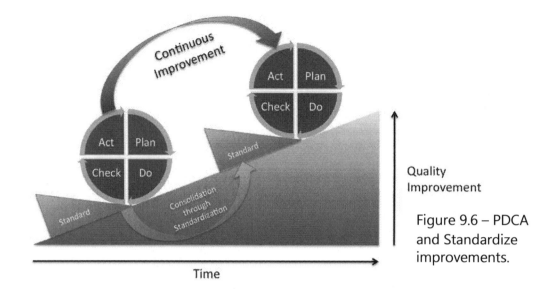

Figure 9.6 – PDCA and Standardize improvements.

H. **Caution – Standard Work that is anchored in clear visual controls (pictures, numbers and colors) is much more sustainable than lengthy written documentation.** How do we keep track of verbal changes in Standard Work? Verbal approaches without documentation are not sustainable, consistent or able to be passed on to other employees accurately.

CHARACTERISTICS OF IDEAL STANDARD WORK[2]:

- Contain as little text as possible
- Use pictures, colors and numbers to attract attention
- Immediately communicate purpose
- No need for interpretation
- Immediately available and visible in the work area
- Do not have to be retrieved from a file
- Do not contain language barriers
- No jargon
- Are better and faster than alternatives
- Workers are happy to use them

VISUAL CONTROLS AND THE VISUAL WORKPLACE

I understand far more by seeing than by reading, hearing, or being told. Of course, actually doing, training and mentoring others is at an even higher level of understanding. The visual workplace approach (Figure 9.7) is another aspect of Standard Work to ensure that gains will be held and sustained with high consistency.

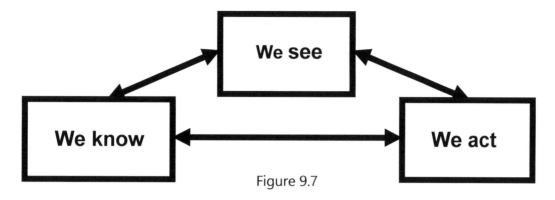

Figure 9.7

What info do I need to know? What info do I need to share/display?

General Guidelines for the Visual Workplace:
- Colors, pictures and numbers work best; use LARGE lettering.
- State information in employee terms.
- Use colors that are visible (watch out for yellow - it's difficult to see on a white background) and be aware of employees who may be color blind.
- Use symbols – thermometers, etc.
- Bar charts work far better than pie charts.
- Use pictures, including employee photos, in the work areas.
- Utilize white boards, flip charts, magnetic boards, team metrics displays.

There are many reference materials available on this subject and we'll list some at the end of this chapter.

The following examples of a visual workplace to ensure Standard Work is sustained (Figures 9.8 and 9.9).

Figure 9.8 Identifying if manuals are missing or in the right sequence

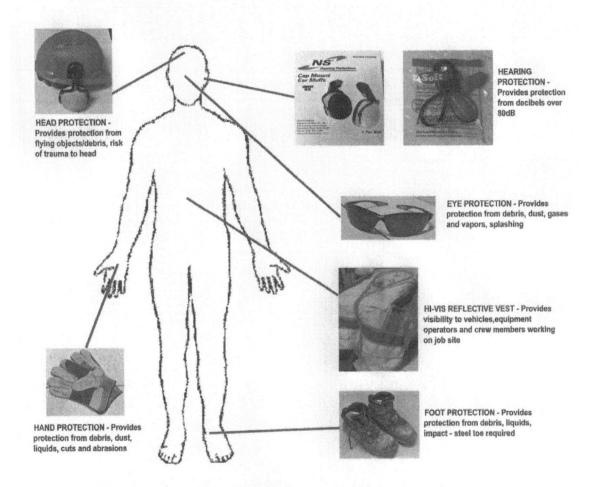

BEFORE YOU LEAVE!
PERSONAL PROTECTIVE EQUIPMENT REQUIREMENTS

HEAD PROTECTION - Provides protection from flying objects/debris, risk of trauma to head

HEARING PROTECTION - Provides protection from decibels over 80dB

EYE PROTECTION - Provides protection from debris, dust, gases and vapors, splashing

HI-VIS REFLECTIVE VEST - Provides visibility to vehicles, equipment operators and crew members working on job site

HAND PROTECTION - Provides protection from debris, dust, liquids, cuts and abrasions

FOOT PROTECTION - Provides protection from debris, liquids, impact - steel toe required

While every job is different, at a minimum you MUST be wearing the basic personal protective equipment shown above. Before you leave this building, make sure you have the required equipment with you or in your vehicle. You must be wearing this at all times on the jobsite. There will be spot checks by your supervisors!

Figure 9.9 Ensuring the correct personal protective equipment is worn (Leesburg, VA)

Do employees have a clear indication of the key metrics and goals and how they are doing?

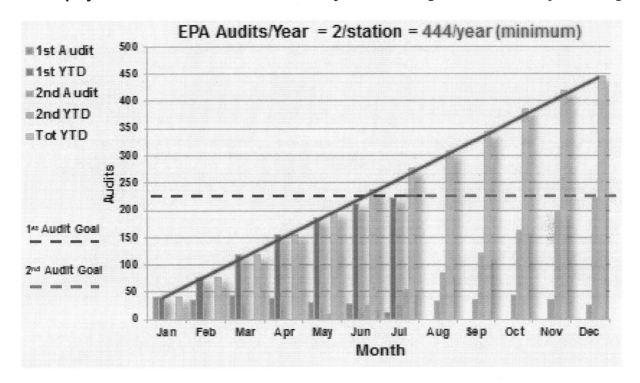

Who's present and where are they at?

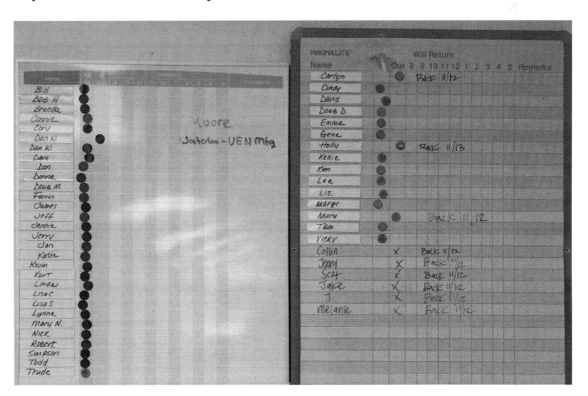

Project Status Board

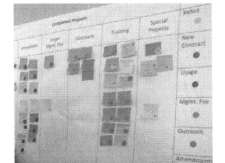

Supplies Cabinet – 5S based

CHAPTER SUMMARY FOR STANDARD WORK: Great Standard Work is fundamental to creating great training and providing greater consistency and less variability in all processes. The supervisor owns the Standard Work. Sustaining the Standard Work and incorporating improvements is one of the hardest things to do in Lean.

REFERENCES:

[1]Crosby, Philip B. (1979). *Quality is Free.* McGraw-Hill.
[2]Robinson, Alan G., and Schroeder, Dean M. (Winter 1993). *Training, Continuous Improvement, and Human Relations: The US TWI Programs and the Japanese Management Style.* California Management Review.
[3]Teeuwen, Bert. (2011). *Lean for the Public Sector: the Pursuit of Perfection in Government Services.* Productivity Press.

REFERENCE MATERIALS FOR STANDARD WORK AND THE VISUAL WORKPLACE:

Liker, Jeffrey K. and Trachlis, George (2016). *Developing Leadership Skills: Module 3 Complete: Standards, Standard Work and Visual Management.* Lean Leadership Institute Publications.
Galsworth, Gwendolyn D. (2013). *Visual thinking: Creating Enterprise Excellence through the Technologies of the Visual Workplace.* Visual-Lean Enterprise Press.

Chapter 10
Project Charter & Project Selection Criteria

How to develop and select what projects should be initiated

A Project Charter is one of the most important documents necessary to get a team started on solid ground. Usually, a first draft of the charter is prepared by the project sponsor. Then, the project team reworks the charter until it is something they feel comfortable owning. At this point, the charter goes back to the sponsor for approval. The project team and sponsor should continue to further clarify the charter as work progresses. It is important that the charter, at all times, reflects the team's best understanding of their work requirement. The Project Charter ensures "we're all on the same page" when undertaking a new project.

Here is an example Project Charter format (Figure 10.1):

Project Name:	Location:
Business Case:	**Problem Statement:**
Why is this project important to the organization strategy and the potential financial impact?	What is wrong, when/where does the problem occur, size of the problem, and impact of the problem?
Project Scope: IN	**Goal:**
Defines the boundaries, constraints, and resources available to the team. Beware of creeping scope during the project.	The quantified results expected to be achieved by the stated date(s).
OUT	**Expected Direct Benefits:** Target
	Projected cost savings
	Expected Indirect Benefits: Target
TEAM: Sponsor/Champion:	Other benefits – cycle time, error rates, etc. reductions, etc.
Leader:	**Total Benefits:**
Facilitator:	
Member	**SPECIAL NOTES:**
Member	
Member	
Member	
Member	
Member	

Figure 10.1

The Project Charter also:
- Clarifies what is expected of the team
- Keeps the team focused
- Keeps the team aligned with organizational priorities
- Transfers the project from the sponsor to the project team leader and team

The elements of the Project Charter (Figure 10.1) are the:
- Problem statement
- Business case
- Goal statement
- Scope
- Estimated direct and indirect benefits
- Sponsor, team leader, and team members

THE PROBLEM STATEMENT – first determine what the problem is:

- What is wrong or not meeting our customers' needs?
- When and where does the problem occur?
- How big is the problem?
- What's the impact of the problem?
- How do you describe the *PAIN*?
- What is the *REAL* Problem?

Key Considerations/Potential Pitfalls when writing the Problem Statement:
- Is the problem based on observation (fact) or assumption (guess)?
- Does the problem statement prejudge a root cause?
- Can data be collected by the team to verify and analyze the problem?
- Is the problem statement too narrowly or broadly defined?
- Is a solution included in the statement?
- Would customers be happy if they knew we were working on this?

Some Problem Statement examples:
O'Fallon, MO: Project Charter: Hiring Process – Reduce the Time to Hire

"It takes too long to fill vacant full time positions and this occurs with all vacancies. The impact is external and internal customer dissatisfaction, work goes undone, morale goes down. When we are short staffed, overtime cost increases. The due diligence in selecting candidates requires a lot of staff time. There is too much paperwork and redundancies in the Personnel Request process. There are also too many approvals needed."

City in Ohio: Project Charter: Request for Services – Work Order Process

"The problem is that there is no centralized place that complaints or work orders originate within the City. In addition, residents do not have the ability to track their complaint or work order to its resolution once it has been submitted. Customers lack education due to inadequate web page and limited use of social media. Not all internal City initial points of contact are trained well enough. There is no electronic info system to effectively manage the work order process. There is a lack of good historical data."

K-12 School District in California: Project Charter: Grants Process

"There is no standardized competitive grants process that encompasses the district and its school sites leading to duplication and wasted efforts by teachers and other district personnel. Communications are not good to parents, teachers, admin & community partners within the process, about the process, and what the benefits are. The problem is both at the district & the school sites. Its magnitude is across all levels of the district. The impact of not doing this: less programs for student support, loss in staffing, loss in district revenue."

BUSINESS CASE: the second element of the Project Charter. Why is this project important to do?

- How will this project drive business initiatives and goals?
- How will this project impact the customer?
- Why is it important to do now? Why is it a priority?
- What are the consequences of not doing it now?
- What are the expected financial benefits?

Some Business Case examples:

A State Social Services Agency: Project Charter: Undeliverable Mail

"Returned mail impacts client services as the client won't receive their mail and/or are not a client anymore and should be closed out. Time is being spent in the agency handling and reconciling mail, although current invalid addresses are not being updated. Eliminating returned mail waste will:
  - *Free up wasted personnel time to do other duties.*
  - *Free up money for postage, copying, and mailing currently spent on waste.*
  - *Better service our client base, creating more value added."*

A State Motor Vehicle Department: Project Charter: International Registration Plan for Interstate Truck Registrations.

"This Project aligns with the following four DMV Strategic Planning Goals:
  - *Improve and enhance Motor Vehicle's core mission functions related to the safety and enforcement of licensing, registry, and motor vehicle-related businesses;*

o *Pursue excellence in the delivery of service and satisfaction to the public through efficient processing of registration applications;*
o *Maximize and enhance the agency's professionalism and organizational performance, to be a "workplace of choice" for its employees; and*
o *Ensure agency compliance with mandates on both a State and Federal level (and DMV compliance with the IRP Plan – an agreement that provides for registration reciprocity).*

"This Project will impact DMV customers/State staff by:
o *Reducing IRP processing and issuance times;*
o *Facilitating more timely transaction flow; and*
o *Providing the foundation for electronic applications and payments.*

"It is important to prioritize this Project for implementation now to provide a timely response to the processing delays identified by the State's motor carrier industry and to address limited staffing by identifying/implementing processes for greater efficiencies.

"The consequences of not conducting this Lean Initiative now include: continued motor carrier industry dissatisfaction; increasing future risks whereby less staff are available and delays become longer; and adverse impacts upon branch offices as carriers request intrastate commercial registrations.

"Expected financial benefits include: reductions in the number of personnel (State IRP and motor carrier) hours required - especially if carrier personnel use the available IRP e-carrier System and electronically enter data; more timely receipt of registration revenues by the State; and reduced business costs to carriers as fewer temporary registrations are obtained."

THE GOAL STATEMENT:

- Defines the improvement the team is seeking to accomplish.
- Starts with a verb (e.g., reduce, eliminate, control, increase, etc.).
- Tends to start broadly—eventually should include measurable target and completion date.
- Must not assign blame, presume cause, or prescribe a solution.

The Goal Statement defines the team's improvement objective

Some Goal Statement examples:

A State Department of Revenue Agency: Project Charter: Undeliverable Mail
o *Reduce client returned mail from over 4% to under 1.5%*
o *Reduce the number of daily notices sent out by 10%*
o *Have annualized cost savings in excess of $250,000 within 6 months of the Kaizen project report out.*

O'Fallon, MO: Project Charter: Hiring Process – Reduce the Time to Hire.
- o   *Reduce the time to fill positions by 50% (specific days before and after were listed)*

THE PROJECT SCOPE:

- What process will the team focus on?
- What are the boundaries of the process we are to improve? What are the starting and stopping points?
- What resources are available to the team?
- What (if anything) is out of bounds for the team?
- What (if any) constraints must the team work under?
- What is the time commitment expected of team members? What will happen to their "regular jobs" while they are doing the project?

PROJECT SELECTION:

A project selection matrix should be developed to prioritize which projects should be chosen with the greatest leverage. There is an extensive set of criteria listed based on Ease, Benefits, and Urgency (Figures 10.2 and 10.3) to establish a project rating grid:

Prioritization Considerations – Urgency	Prioritization Considerations – Urgency
• **Degree** 　　High—Have to do 　　Medium—Need to do 　　*Low—Should* do • **Type** 　　Internal vs. external 　　Proactive (ongoing improvement) vs. reactive (responding to new discoveries or conditions) 　　Threat vs. opportunity	• **Initiator/Driver—People** 　　Customers 　　Supplier 　　Workforce 　　External stakeholders • **Initiator/Driver—Conditions** 　　Market 　　Financial 　　Operational 　　Regulatory/legal 　　Environmental/political

Figure 10.2

Prioritization Considerations - Ease	Prioritization Considerations – Benefits

Investment required
  Time
  Money
 	
Resource availability
  People
  Equipment & material
 	
Logistics
  Physical location
  Space & storage
  Travel/transportation
 	
External stakeholders
  Customers/ constituents
  Suppliers
  Unions
  Regulatory agencies
  Boards
 	
Potential disruption
  Internal, external
  Operational, financial
 	
Market considerations
  Customers
  Competitors
  Supply base
	Customers/market
	  Higher quality/safety
	  Faster delivery
	  Lower prices
	  Greater market share
	  Better innovation
	
	Financial
	  Lower expenses
	  Higher revenue
	  Faster cash flow
	  Lower debt burden
	
	Employees
	  More fulfilling work
	  Better environment
	  Safer conditions
	  Higher retention
	  Easier recruiting
	
	Operational
	  Greater flow
	  Increased productivity
	  Better equipment reliability
	  Rationalized supply chain
	  Greater scalability
	  Regulatory/Legal
	  Lower compliance risk
	  Lower litigation risk
	
	Organizational
	  More profitable
	  Greater agility
	  Better reputation
	  Enhanced predictability

Figure 10.3

Process Improvement
Project Selection Matrix Example

Requested Projects	Strategic Importance /Impact on Dept Objectives	Financial Impact	Source of Customer Dissatisfaction	Visibility of Positive Results	Time to Implement	Resources Needed	Probability of Creating New Problems	Sum Across of the Ratings
	5 Major 4 Significant 3 High 2 Moderate 1 Low 0 Very Little	5 Major 4 Significant 3 High 2 Moderate 1 Low 0 Very little	5 Major 4 Significant 3 High 2 Moderate 1 Low 0 Very little	5 Very Clear 4 Clear 3 Some Indic 2 Few Indic 1 Hard to See 0 Intangible	5 Almost Immed 4 < One Month 3 1-2 Months 2 3-4 Months 1 5-6 Months 0 > 6 Months	5 Almost Nil 4 Few 3 Modest 2 Moderate 1 Considerable 0 Major	5 Very Low 4 Low Risk 3 Some Poss. 2 Mod. Poss. 1 Probable 0 Almost Certain	

Figure 10.4

This is a training example (Figure 10.4 - in real life the criteria would be more quantitative/specific). Developing a category such as Financial Impact:

5 Major --   Direct savings of at least $500K and/or indirect savings of at least $1,000,000
4 Significant -- Direct savings $250K to $499 and/or indirect savings of $500K to $999K
3 High -- Direct savings $100K to $249K and/or indirect savings of $250K to $499K
2 Moderate -- Direct savings of $50K to $99K and/or indirect savings of $100K to $249K
1 Low -- Direct savings of $25K to $49K and/or indirect savings of $50K to $99K

The proposed projects, with Project Charters provided, would be listed in the left hand column. Then each project would be rated in each of the columns. The total scores could be added up or multiplied (if this is the case, having a 0 level in any one column would multiple out to 0 for a total score, so use a 1-5 rating grid) across each row to determine a final score. The highest-rated projects would be the most logical candidates for new project teams.

The following are examples from California and Connecticut who generated criteria for Lean Government metrics and benefits:

Metrics/Benefits for Project Charters – Eureka Institute – State of California[1]:

Lean Metrics Reference Guide

Performance metrics help to gauge the effectives of a program's strategies to achieve an agency's goals. There is not one perfect set of metrics - the "right" metrics will depend on the project's goals and may require multiple iterations to discover more about the process in question. In general, good metrics:

- Are related to the program's goals and purpose
- Provide a reliable measurement of outputs and outcomes
- Help determine gaps between goals and reality
- Guide program improvement

It is helpful to focus on a mix of metrics that measure different aspects of the service being provided - for example, use one metric that is meaningful to the customer and another that addresses the organizational goals for the leaders.

Metrics can be difficult to grasp. Trying to focus on just four metric categories to help you establish a current state and a target future state and allows metrics to drive the MEAT of your improvements.

Money	Errors	Amounts	Time
• What is the cost of your process? • Hard Costs = cost for things • Soft Costs = cost for labor	• How much rework? • How many additional steps to fix? • How many defects?	• How many do you produce? • How many are ordered? • How many jobs are "work in progress"?	• How long does it take to produce? • Is there a wait time? • How many approvals?

Lean Metrics Reference Guide

As the California Lean Academy begins to document how its participants' are impacting their work processes and delivering better services to the public the following MEAT metrics are of particular interest:

	Metric	Definition
ERRORS	Defect Rate	Percent of services or products that are "defective"
	Rework Steps/Time	Amount of steps/time to correct mistakes or get missing information
	Percent Complete & Accurate	Percent of occurrences when a step is completed without needing corrections or requesting missing information
	Rolling First-Time Yield	Percent of occurrences where the entire process is completed without rework
AMOUNTS	Handoffs	Number of times the service or product changes hands
	Backlog	Number of service requests or products waiting to start the process
	Process Steps	Number of steps to complete a process
TIME	Lead Time	Total time from start to finish to deliver a service or product to the customer, including wait time
	Processing Time	Amount of time spent on process steps, not including wait time
	Response Time	Amount of time to respond to a customer request for a service or product
	% On Time Delivery	Percent of time the service or product is delivered on time

Note: not all of these metrics may apply and the "right" metrics will depend on how appropriate, applicable and useful for your improvement goals.

Once you determine the appropriate metrics to use, list your metrics in boxes P2 and P3 of the A3 template. List the MEAT for the current state in box P2, and list how your agency would ideally like those same measures to be in the future state in box P3.

Lean Metrics Reference Guide

An example: An agency is trying to improve their work order process. They know how many work orders are requested through their system, how long (on average) it takes to process a work order, and how many are successfully processed correctly the first time. Using this information, they can calculate how much it costs their agency to complete this process. The metrics are listed in the A3 format below:

P2 | Current State

- Money: 100 work orders/month X **10** hours/work order X $25/hour = $25,000 + 1,250 in rework costs (5 reworked X 10 hours X $25) = **$26, 250 Total**
- Errors: 5% completed incorrectly and must be reworked; average customer quality rating of 3.5/5
- Amounts: Complete 100 work orders/month
- Time: Average time to complete a work order = 10 hours

P3 | Future State

- Money: 100 work orders/month X **8.5** hours/work order X $25/hour = $21,250 + $0 in rework costs = **$21,250 Total**
- Errors: 0% completed incorrectly; average customer quality rating of 4.5/5
- Amounts: Complete 100 work orders/month
- Time: Average time to complete a work order = 8.5 hours

As you implement and monitor, these metrics are entered in C6 of the A3 to show the actual results of your improvements as noted below:

C6 | Results

P2	P3	30 Days	60 Days	90 Days
•M = $26,250 •E = 5% error rate •A = 100 w.o./month •T = 10 hours/w.o.	•M = $21,250 •E = 0% error rate •A = 100 w.o./month •T = 8.5 hours/w.o.	•M = $24,462 •E = 3% error rate •A = 100 W.O./month •T = 9.5 hours/w.o.	•M = 22,725 •E = 1% error rate •A = 100 w.o./month •T = 9 hours/w.o.	•M = $21,875 •E = 0% error rate •A = 100 w.o./month •T = 8.75 hours/w.o.

As you track your projects' progress, please also submit the **CA LEAN RESULTS REPORT**. This will allow the CA Lean Academy to highlight statewide Lean successes!

An example from the State of Connecticut[2] of areas where savings can be developed from:

Lean Metrics Guide

Time	Cost	Quality
How long does it take to deliver a service/respond to a request? How much of that time is "value-added"?	How much does the process cost to operate? Is there a savings or a revenue impact associated with the proposed changes?	How often does the current process lead to rework, dissatisfaction, recidivism, etc.?
• Lead time for the process (total time from start to finish with project scope) • Percent on-time (based on goals set by statute or by agency/department leadership) • Processing time (excludes wait time) • Activity Ratio (% = Processing time/Lead time) • Value added time • Percent value added time • Non-value added time • Non-value added but necessary time (statutory or regulatory obligation)	• Cost avoidance savings • Resources spent on mission-critical activity (pre and post implementing changes) • Cost per service or process (including direct and indirect costs) • Revenue impact	• Customer satisfaction – surveys or complaint data • Percent of process that requires rework/Total number of reworked steps • Percent complete and accurate (does not require corrections or rework) • Recidivism rate • Frequency of similar issues reoccurring
Productivity/Output	**Organization/Workforce**	**Process/Takt**
How much was produced (daily, weekly, monthly, or annually)? Will this quantity increase or decrease with the proposed changes?	How can we create a workforce that is safe, skilled and satisfied within a culture of continuous improvement?	These metrics will likely occur during the analysis, but should continue to be measured as part of P-D-C-A.
• Backlog • Excess inventory • Amount of output produced (e.g. applications) in a given period of time • Effectiveness (actual output/planned output) • Amount of output produced (e.g. applications) by staffing level • Number of databases/systems	• Safety/Workers' Compensation (claims/100 FTEs) • Retention rate • Percent of staff trained in core competency areas (job or classification specific) • Percent of staff trained in Lean tools or principles • Status of Continuous Improvement Strategic Plan • Number of Kaizen events conducted • Percent of staff exposed to "Lean thinking" (Number of project ideas/total staff)	• Total process steps • Value added process steps • Non-value added process steps • Transport time • Wait time • Rework/Loop backs • Barriers

LeanCT

PROJECT CHARTER AND SELECTION CRITERIA SUMMARY: Project Charters ensure that efforts are made to develop the value-added case for doing a project. Projects can be rushed into based on emotions and opinions or spontaneous reactions and be very unproductive. Developing a good Project Charter coupled with a solid project selection process creates the best opportunities for success.

REFERENCES FOR PROJECT SELECTION CRITERIA

[1]State of California Eureka Institute: **https://www.govops.ca.gov/wp-content/uploads/sites/11/2017/04/Lean-Metrics-Reference-Guide.pdf**
[2]State of Connecticut Metrics Guide: **http://www.ct.gov/opm/lib/opm/LeanCT_Metrics_Guide.pdf**

Chapter 11
Kaizen

Continuous improvement must be continuously done.

This chapter will address Kaizen in two contexts:

1. The Kaizen (Rapid Improvement) event, which is usually three to five full-time days long, focused on a high-leverage process improvement project. Most Government Lean efforts are focused here along with applying the other Lean tools. Only applying Lean tools, however, does not drive or guarantee a Lean culture.

2. Daily Kaizen is focused on harnessing the collective skills and ideas of all employees to create daily improvements that usually are small in nature but cumulatively create a true Lean culture.

"Employee Ideas are key to building a culture of high performance." Alan G. Robinson and Dean M. Schroeder[1]

KAIZEN (RAPID IMPROVEMENT) EVENTS

Kaizen events build on the content of previous chapters. A project sponsor decides there is a need to create a preliminary project charter to address a problem or improvement opportunity. The project charter would then go to a Lean steering committee to decide if the project should be resourced by using a project selection grid or some other form of determining the leverage-effort benefit of the project. Top opportunities get approved and the preliminary pre-work begins.

KAIZEN EVENT PREPARATION STANDARD WORK

Pre-event Data Collection Steps

1. Initial map of the current process developed by the team that is going through the Kaizen event.
2. Determine from the map steps what can and cannot be changed and identify those steps that are mandatory by rule or statute (must be factual).
3. Outline what items are currently tracked for time.
4. For those items currently tracked for time, determine longest item, quickest item and an average of the items. Do not try to gather data here that you do not already know.
5. Have the staff write down what they do for a week. This includes the projects, as well as meetings, site visits, telephone calls, regular meetings, etc.

The "Voice of the Customer" Data Considerations

A key area of data collection is gathering "Voice of the Customer" information. Some questions to ask as part of the "voice of the customer" are the following:

1. What do they want?
2. When do they want it?
3. Why do they want it?
4. How do they use the product/service and how much of it do they use?

These questions will ultimately help in determining the "value-added" steps in the process, as well as provide potential design criteria for the final product. The best approach would be to ask the customers (select a few) or at least think through these questions from their perspective. Customer surveys and focus groups can also be utilized (see Chapter 4 on Customers). If the process has different customer segments, then questions could be asked for each one. This information would be useful for goal-setting purposes.

Benchmarking would also be helpful in establishing goals for the event. Additionally, it could equip the team with example strategies for achieving the goals for the event.

POTENTIAL BASELINE METRICS COULD INCLUDE:

- Number of process steps
- Total lead time
- Data on staffing needs
- Data on staff time
- Cycle time
- Data on transaction volume in process (e.g., number of applications)
- Number of handoffs
- Amount of backlog
- Rework/error percentage (e.g., percent of permits needing rework)

Go/No-Go Kaizen Event Checklist
This checklist covers all the steps that are necessary to get a Kaizen event set up for success.

Is the scope complete and appropriately sized?
- A preliminary Project Charter has been done by the Sponsor/Champion (It is ideal to also have a preliminary Elevator Speech and Stakeholder Analysis done beforehand.)
- Is the scope too large to achieve success? (Don't try to boil the ocean.)
- Is the scope so small success will not be transformational? (Don't expend this kind of time and energy unless you can achieve significant results -- at least a 50% improvement.)
- Are you improving a complete value stream instead of putting bandages on parts of the process?
- Is there any information or decisions made about future plans, "sacred cows," or past or potential problems the team needs to understand to be fully empowered to implement change?

Are the right people on the team?
- Do you have all the areas of the process being improved represented?
- Do you have the horsepower needed to make critical decisions?
- Do you have customers on the team (optional) or, in unusual cases; have you surveyed or discussed the event with process users so the "voice of the customer" is represented?
- Have you included thoughtful, good organizational thinkers with little or no knowledge of the process to provide a fresh perspective?
- Are the team members strong, well-respected, knowledgeable employees and not the people you can most afford to do without for a week?
- Team size (normally 6-8) – follow governance training modules for who should be the:
  o Team sponsor/champion
  o Team leader
  o Team members

Is the necessary data and information available to ensure and measure success?
- If there was a data gathering plan developed, has the information been collected?
- What is the baseline real data – how are we doing?

Are we ready to immediately implement significant improvements and changes?
- Are there decisions to be made by management before the team can implement change?
- Is there a strong mandate to do things differently the following Monday?

Is the event a top priority for that week?
- Is the entire team committed and scheduled to spend the full week focused on the event?
- Are the same adequate-sized large room and breakout rooms available the entire week?

- Is the team leader committed to change, available all week and able to put in the time before, during and after the event to ensure success?
- Are subject matter experts able to be on "stand-by" to support the team as needed?
- Is the sponsor committed to implementing the results and available to help remove barriers during the course of the week?

Is there a common understanding and commitment about the Kaizen event process?
- Is there an understanding that the team is not just making recommendations, but will make decisions in consultation with management during the week that will begin to be implemented immediately?
- Are all levels of the organization (management, unions, and affected workers) aware of the Kaizen event and understand that there will be significant changes coming?
- Is there a commitment to designing and implementing the best solution and improvements for the customer by using data, Lean tools and the process?

Have the potential regulatory and contractual issues been researched beforehand?
- Are there State or Federal statutes/regulations that impact the project?
- What existing contracts relate to the project?
- Are there any agreements of understanding (MOUs/MOAs) with unions or other entities?
- What forms, policies and procedures need to be reviewed?

Have you benchmarked other city/agencies for their similar value streams/processes?
- Benchmarking establishes learning from others and best practices.
- It establishes a higher baseline to start from and saves time.
- Ask others how they have quantified the benefits.

Have communications been done?
- Project team members have the preliminary charter and event Elevator Speech beforehand.
- All team members' supervisors are informed at least two weeks in advance before their employees (team members) are informed of the event (at least one week in advance).
- Any Kaizen event-affected areas are given the initial Elevator Speech (verbally and through copies) a week before the Kaizen event to minimize concerns.

This preliminary preparation work is done by the project sponsor/champion with the team leader and any other necessary resources able to capture the Kaizen event preparation work. The checklist:

Kaizen (Rapid Improvement) Event Checklist

☐ All supervisors of team members informed.
☐ All team members informed beforehand with preliminary Elevator Speech.

- [ ] All affected areas informed beforehand with preliminary Elevator Speech.
- [ ] All Kaizen team members are there full time and not to be taken out of the event.
- [ ] All participants should bring a pad and pen and/or be provided these.
- [ ] Sufficient sized room available/dedicated for the entire event duration with large wall space for posting maps.
- [ ] Event report out set for top management on last event day at 3PM.
- [ ] Initial data mining done.
- [ ] Initial benchmarking done.
- [ ] Copy of any relevant ordinances, statutes or laws.
- [ ] Copy of initial project charter and elevator speech for everyone.
- [ ] Dress is business casual.

We are now ready for the Kaizen event to begin. The Kaizen event outline is for a consecutive five-day full-time event (Figure 11.1).

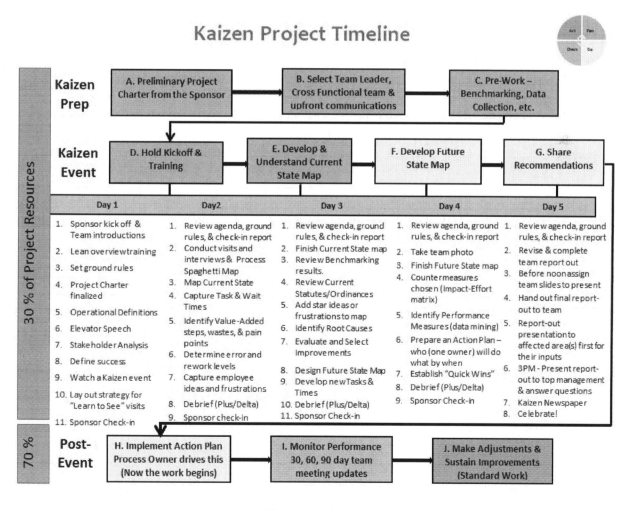

Figure 11.1

KAIZEN EVENT STANDARD WORK (FOR THE ACTUAL EVENT)

Logistics:

1. Conference room/site (large enough) dedicated for the week – don't keep bouncing from site to site.
2. 8:30-4:30 is normal, one break in AM, breaks in PM determined by pace, etc.; lunch should not exceed 45 minutes.
3. Have sponsor/champion kick off day one and show up at the end of each day for a "reality check".
4. Ensure all team members and their supervisors are communicated to about the event at least one week in advance, including an Elevator Speech.
5. Top management is invited well in advance to the 3PM fifth day (Friday) top management report out.

DAY ONE:

1. Start the day with everyone briefly introducing themselves and their expectations for the Kaizen event.
2. Cover guidelines if a cell phone goes off or someone is late (have fun with this).
3. Briefly cover the Lean facilitator's background info. The facilitator is the person who is coordinating and leading the Kaizen event.
4. Go through all of the training in day one, including all the work areas, and cover what each of the five days will look like.
5. Output from day one:
   a. Project charter is discussed and almost finalized (there may be some changes during the week). A large amount of time is spent on truly defining the problem; have the word document for the project charter on the screen and modify electronically – first night – load up into the Kaizen report out template.
   b. Operational definitions are done (could be modified or added to later).
   c. Final Elevator Speech is done (one volunteer to wordsmith the team input that night for the team for the next day).
   d. Stakeholder Analysis is done with strategies needing to be flushed out further (later in the week the Stakeholder Analysis may be further refined) – understand if there are some folks that will be directly impacted and decide if there needs to be several brief communications to those individuals or groups as the week progresses.
   e. Project goal and benefits are discussed and captured. Have a good "challenge" for the team; 50%, or more, challenge improvement targets are normal.
   f. Lay out strategy for "learning to see" visits or interviews for day two.
   g. Discuss the current state process understanding, if time allows.
   h. Show a Kaizen event output example from a past event so the team sees what it looks like.
   i. Day one evening – populate the Kaizen template based on day one outputs.

DAY TWO: Have a camera with you – cell phones can be used to time operations

1. Ask the team what they learned from day one.
2. Teams go out and conduct "learn to see" interviews.
   a. Remind them what the interviews are all about and how to conduct them.
      i. In some cases, large projects and/or multiple sites may require interviews to be done beforehand.
      ii. Set an interview schedule for the day and make sure each team can contact the other about progress via cell phones.
      iii. Come back together at lunch time to do a reality check on how things are going and the same for 4PM.
   b. Interview teams should NEVER have all members who really know the process on one team – this is much less effective. On an interview team, balance a knowledgeable person with someone who doesn't know – they ask great questions. The knowledgeable person already "knows" what is happening and will jump over stuff or assume what is happening
   c. Be sure to ask/look for errors and rework – they're always there and larger than they know.
   d. Always ask or look for data – convert opinion to fact; estimates are the absolute last resort.
   e. Ensure people are numbering each sequence of the work and capturing all of the items of the process that are being done (Value Stream [VS] Data Collection sheet).
   f. Teams can use sticky notes with color coding as long as they capture the complete process and number the notes in sequence. Some use note pads and some use the VS Data Collection sheet. Ensure process sequence rigor is maintained.
   g. Take a picture of everyone interviewed – they will be acknowledged in the report out; always ask first for permission (use a mini Elevator Speech, if necessary).
   h. Take pictures of the process if there are interesting areas, 5S opportunities, etc.
   i. Spaghetti map the process – distances traveled (steps = feet), locations, etc.
   j. Current State (Swim Lane) mapping has been transferred from the sticky notes on the wall to Visio – you may be doing this the evening of the second day or third day.
   k. If not Visio mapped, then everything would be on flipchart paper (or rolled paper) and Swim Lane mapped on the wall (admittedly, this uses quite a bit of space) and then take pictures. Later, someone on the team will need to capture the paper data and put it into electronic form (Visio is best).
3. Always think about how things are balanced; make sure the folks on the team are gainfully doing value added team activities. Split the team up to focus on multiple tasks.
4. Lay out the team plan for day three.
5. Output from day two:
   a. Interviews may need to continue for AM of day three
   b. Do current state process map in Visio (desired) evening of day two
   c. Plan for day three schedule
   d. Spaghetti Map
   e. Update Kaizen report out template and do a reality check on status

Value Stream Mapping Guidelines

1. The Swim Lane Map is the approach that seems to work best for Government.
2. Project Charter: What is the goal of the project? Have the team discuss and reach agreement (the goal could change over the course of the Kaizen); this drives the future state.
3. Clear Operational Definitions:
    a. Start point of the process
    b. End of the process
    c. Other key definitions for team and viewer clarity
4. Depending on team size and process complexity, go "learn to see":
    a. Break up the team: one group start at the process beginning and the other starts at the end and works backwards until they meet. This means that if you work at the end, you interview that process step in the sequence that they do their work
    b. Extensive interviewing. Use VSM data collection sheet (Chapter 8) and sticky notes; number each sticky note in the process sequence and gather all info at that process step. Put green dots on sticky note with VA and red dots for NVA.
    c. If it's a simple process, make sure you know what else needs to be accomplished, so some of the team could be "learning to see" and others could be doing data mining, Elevator Speech clean up, etc. "Divide and conquer" to ensure everyone has something to do to contribute to the Kaizen report out template.
5. After "learning to see," assemble the team and set up a Swim Lane map (as many flip chart sheets as you need on the wall or a roll of butcher block paper or 36-inch-wide paper). Put all current state process info (sticky notes, data collection sheets, forms, computer screen prints, errors, rework, reports, ideas and frustrations) and plot from start to end of the process.
6. Have everyone continue to provide input to ensure as much info on the current state is captured and continue to populate the Swim Lane with ideas (stars sticky symbols) that come up.
7. Take pictures of final current state Swim Lane map or put on Visio (ideal).
8. Note: The Current State learning and map is usually done by noon on the third day of the event.
9. Test out as many improvements (PDCA) as you can during the event. Action items should be assigned – who will do what by when. Put ideas on an impact-effort grid (Figure 11.2). Work on high-impact, low-effort action items first.

DAY THREE:

1. Ask team members what they learned from day two
2. Set a plan and strategy for day three. Current state mapping should be done NO LATER THAN NOON on day 3, including all VA and NVA data capturing – times, errors/rework, reports, WIP, etc.

3. Review Kaizen report out template open items with team just before or after lunch.
4. Review all VA and NVA steps and capture.
5. Start to construct a desired Future State Map (Swim Lane).
6. Have Impact-Effort matrix up for ideas to be posted there (Figure 11.2).
7. Further develop communications strategy for stakeholders.
8. Implement "quick wins" that are obvious and easy to do.
9. Then, develop ideal future state map with ideas or action items. Take pictures of future state map or put on Visio (ideal).

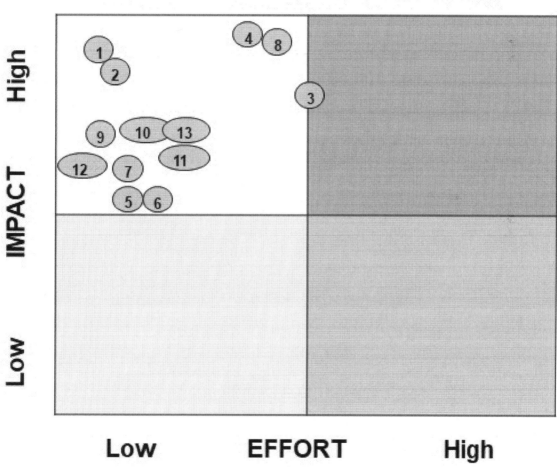

Figure 11.2 - Circled numbers are action items

DAY FOUR:
1. Review learning from day three.
2. Review template and action items for day four (desired state at the end of day four):
   a. Future State Map is done (preferably Visio) and reworked/improved.

   b. Countermeasures are collected and chosen (Impact-Effort matrix). Establish who will do what and by when.

   c. Continue appropriate data mining to generate facts.

   d. Print a copy of the template for all to see by noon of day four as a working document and continue to "fill in the blanks" on day four.

DAY FIVE:

1. Review learning from day four.
2. Continue to refine the Kaizen template.
3. Capture Kaizen lessons learned for the template (late morning).
4. Before noon, decide who will do what slides for the team report out – all team members should present some slide(s).
5. Generate copies of the final report out to team members.
6. Kaizen newspaper action items (see below) completed – for open items going forward, who will be doing what by when (their personal commitment date). Action items have one owner (not a team).
7. Practice the team presentation around lunch time (before, during or after, depending on the team's process stage).
8. Present report out to any directly affected group after lunch (first presentation). They will ask questions and possibly point out something that was missed or is in error. This also helps build the understanding of the recommended changes with this key stakeholder group.
9. Top management report out to be done at 3PM
   a. The report out shows what the team has done - audience Q&A at the end.
   b. Another important purpose of the report out is to further educate the audience about Lean and further stimulate their thinking on other areas where it also could be applied
   c. Celebrate success. And get Kaizen event feedback forms back.

KAIZEN NEWSPAPER GUIDELINES

- Publish what was accomplished during the Kaizen event.
- Include remaining open action items – who will do what by when.
- Post visibly in actual Kaizen event and process owner's area and update as action items are completed.
- Issue updates at the end of each month until all action items are completed.
- Post Kaizen metric in a prominent location where the process owner is located.

To clarify these items:

1. Specific times, actions and individual action item owners should be clear.
2. Actions are in one-month timeframe objectives. If it's deemed that an action item will take several months to complete, then monthly milestone elements should be determined to meet the overall action item.

3. The monthly Kaizen newspaper updates should be issued within a maximum one week of the end of each month, or sooner.
4. The process owner is responsible for issuing the Kaizen newspaper and the Project Sponsor/Champion is responsible for ensuring this happens.

The core elements for a Kaizen standard report out template normally include the following:

1. Project team title and picture with project sponsor
2. Special thanks to employees who were interviewed and provided inputs to the Kaizen team. Acknowledge them with their pictures, if possible
3. Customer needs
4. Finalized Project Charter
5. Project Financial Benefits and Goals
6. Project Elevator Speech for communications
7. Stakeholder Analysis for Change Management
8. Operational Definitions
9. Data Mining Inputs
10. Value Stream Process mapping of the current state with extensive details
11. Legal issues or constraints -- Does the process accurately follow the legal requirements?
12. Benchmarking results
13. Spaghetti Work Flow Map
14. Findings - Value Added and Non Value Added
15. Standard Work sheets and Standard Work development plans
16. Future State Process Map
17. Comparison grid between current and future state – process overall time, process steps, distances, etc.
18. Quick Win improvements implemented
19. Impact/Effort Matrix for changes to be implemented
20. Measure What Matters – the key process indicator(KPIs) to monitor the process improvements and hold the gains
21. Visual controls and mistake proofing to hold the gains
22. Examples of 5S, checklists, concentration diagrams, and forms/instructions design
23. Kaizen Newspaper – who is doing what by when and forward plans in monthly increments. The Kaizen team leader usually becomes the Kaizen process owner after the event and schedules monthly team follow-up meetings to track implementation progress.
24. Kaizen team lessons learned
25. Other inputs appropriate to the specific project

Team members love Kaizen events because many action items have immediate impact and they feel empowered. A frequent question that is asked is "why can't we work like this all the time (making improvements)?"

DAILY KAIZEN

Daily Kaizen is the generation of continuous improvement ideas by employees on a daily basis. The two major ways this is accomplished is through daily team huddles and employee Dynamic Idea Generation (DIG).

DAILY HUDDLES

Figure 11.3

- Huddles should become a key part of daily management activities (Figure 11.3). Huddles are 15-20 minutes in duration at the beginning of the work day.
- They are stand up (no sitting) and held in the team metrics area. Doing stand-up meetings reduces the meeting time and increases huddle effectiveness.
- Huddle agenda items could cover: process or project status, metrics review and action assignments, problems encountered in the last 24 hours, collective learnings to share, ideas for improvements, upcoming events or visits, general organization information sharing, items to be integrated into standard work, and other appropriate items. Issues are raised and communicated as they occur, minimizing issues from becoming larger.
- Key action items are captured, owners assigned and posted, if necessary.
- Many teams rotate the daily huddle leader so everyone has a chance to lead the team.

Huddle Goals:

- o Work together toward continuous improvements.
- o Draw out everyone's ideas, especially the folks who do the job.
- Huddles improve morale and achieving goals.

Huddle Guiding Principles:
- Have a "can do" attitude.
- Start and end on time.
- Respect every individual – focus on the process.
- Identify the root cause of the problem.
- Focus on dynamic data-based decision making from the process daily data.
- The targets are a minimum 50%+ improvements.
- Improvements must be integrated into standard work.

DYNAMIC IDEA GENERATION (DIG)

DIG was adopted and adapted from the books written by Robinson and Schroeder[1]. The main difference between DIG and a traditional suggestion system is the degree of employee ownership. DIG is for smaller ideas that are easier to implement, provided they are worth doing. Each of the following idea forms (Figures 11.4-6) are initiated and filled out by the employee who had the idea. The ownership, development and implementation of the idea is handled by the employee.

> **Dynamic Idea Generation (DIG)**
> **What is the Problem?**
>
> **My idea is:**
>
> **How does this help? (The Business Case):**
>
> **Implementation Sequence:**
>
> **Benefit/Savings ($, Time, etc.):**
>
> **Owner:**   **Date:**

Figure 11.4 - A simple Idea form.

An idea form used at Virginia Mason Hospital in Seattle, WA (Figure 11.5):

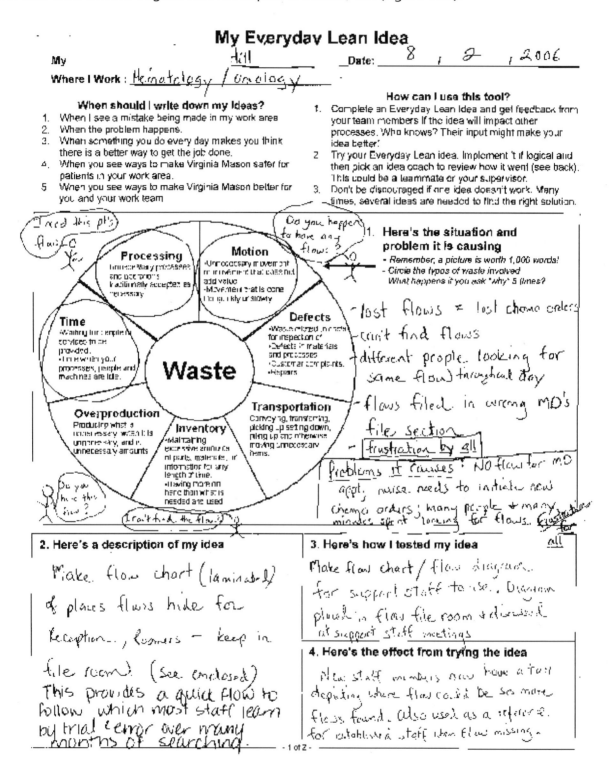

Figure 11.5

A similar idea form (front and back side shown - Chris Lindstrom - Ceptara Corporation) (Figure 11.6):

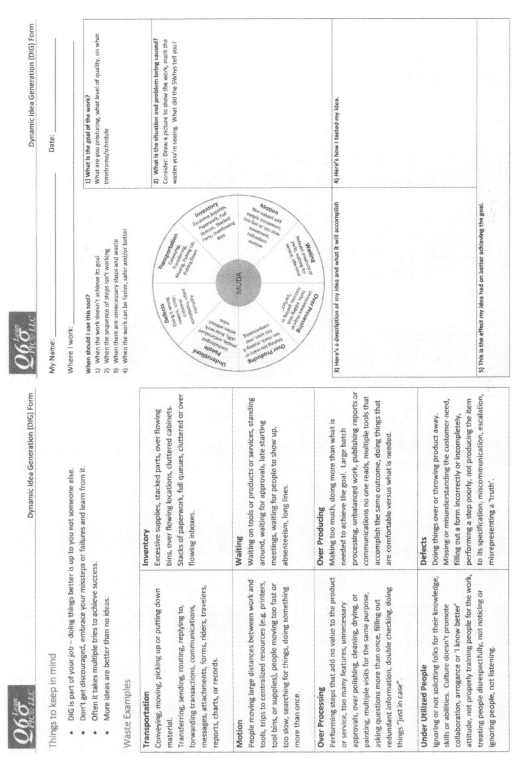

Figure 11.6

Ideas are then posted in the work area for everyone to see (Figures 11.7 and 11.8). This leads to inputs to build on the idea from other team members, other team members being stimulated to have other new ideas, and encourage team members buy in on the idea.

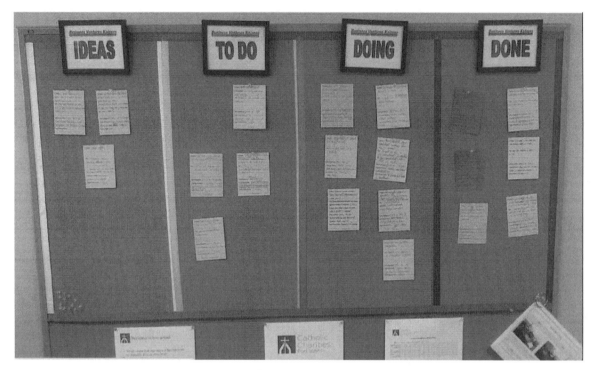

Figure 11.7

Another posting example of employee ideas in the team work area:

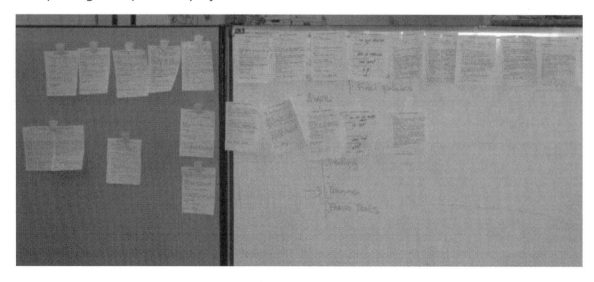

Figure 11.8

Caution on verbal ideas: Verbal ideas are difficult to pass on to others, implement, do consistently and remember. They must be implemented in Standard Work clearly written instructions (such as TWI – Training Within Industry), supplemented by area visual controls and permanent physical changes.

DIG seems pretty easy to do, but before charging forward and creating a disaster, it's important to understand some steps that should be followed.

The Executive Leader's role:
- Ensure that everyone understands that ideas are important and expected to be managed effectively.
- Goes to the Gemba (work area) to ask employees how ideas are being handled.
- Reviews metrics to ensure the idea system is working well, such as:
  o Number of ideas per month or quarter
  o Number of ideas per employee
  o Speed of idea decisions and implementation
  o Concentration diagrams where ideas originate

The Middle Manager's Role:
- To make sure the necessary resources are available to evaluate, test and implement the ideas and provide the necessary training.
- They must also oversee the process in their units and get personally involved with the more significant ideas.
- Address any idea process bottlenecks.

The Team Supervisor's Role:
- Treat everyone with dignity and respect. Make it easy for employees to come forward to ask questions and discuss their ideas. This is key.
- To create an environment that encourages ideas.
- To help employees develop their knowledge and improve their problem-solving skills in order to increase the quality and impact of their ideas
- To champion ideas and look for larger possible implications in them.
- The four key supervisory roles are encouraging ideas, mentoring ideas, championing ideas and looking to build on and leverage submitted ideas.

How to solicit employee ideas:
- Ask your people for their ideas. Target a specific issue or theme on which to concentrate idea generation. Remember that There are no bad ideas; they're learning opportunities. Expect ideas from everyone.
- What ideas are generated for a current change that is impacting the organization?

- What type of problems exist?
- What frustrates you about your job? What would make your job easier to do?
- What types of wastes are identified?
- What do you see?
- How can we do something better, faster or cheaper?
- How can we better serve our customers?

Go after small ideas:

- Small ideas are where most of the improvement, innovation and action resides – and they are off the leadership radar screen ("learn to see").
- Small ideas are much easier to implement because of:
  o less resistance,
  o lower risk – better for learning, and
  o easier review, acceptance and getting them done.

Key points for effective idea generation and implementation:

- Ideas are part of normal work.
- Ideas are easy to submit.
- Ideas are reviewed and discussed by people with direct knowledge, who will be affected, and who can build on or modify the idea.
- Decision making is rapid, effective and efficient.
- Feedback to the suggester is quick and complete – the person is present in the room.
- Ideas are immediately implemented and incorporated into standard work.

Elements of a Good Idea Process:

- Have a forum to discuss ideas within the workgroup before going anywhere else.
- When it comes to problems and opportunities, make sure to consider other options besides the proposed idea.
- Decision making and implementation should be at the lowest level possible.
- Ensure adequate resources can support the ideas; otherwise the idea process will falter.
- Have an effective escalation process for completed work.

Criteria for Qualifying Ideas:

- Safety – this is paramount.
- Work related – a key theme.
- Quality – can't be compromised and should be enhanced.
- Simplicity – the simpler, the better and the easier to standardize.
- Speed – it's a faster way.

Establishing an Idea Process:

1. **Do a pilot first – this is critical.** It is, in effect, applying PDCA to the idea process. Pick an area to pilot with a great supervisor and a positive team. Then go through the previous guidelines and these subsequent steps to observe and learn. A sponsor should have oversight of the pilot.

2. **Submitting ideas is simple and easy.** See the previous idea form examples. At Milliken Corporation, for example, every idea is acknowledged in 24 hours and a decision is made within 72 hours (the decision could be for further study).
   - Evaluating ideas must be done quickly and effectively.
   - Make decisions at the lowest level possible.
   - Suggesters make as many decisions as possible about their own ideas after they've done the research.
   - Idea decisions should be made in weekly team meetings.

3. **Feedback is timely, constructive and informative.**
   - Most feedback can be provided orally on the spot.
   - It allows an opportunity for discussion, which can lead to an idea being further refined.
   - Feedback could be posted on area idea boards for review. Then review all ideas in the area at a once a week team meeting.

4. **Implementation of an idea is rapid and smooth:**
   - Be prepared for the "front end" surge in ideas. When the floodgates open up, be ready to deal with it – this is a critical stage when everyone will be watching. Don't bog down or ignore bottlenecks.
   - Resources have to be able to respond.
   - Implementation works better when it's pushed down to the front lines.

5. **Ideas are reviewed for additional potential. Where can they be applied to other problems or opportunities?** This can be via:
   - Organization intranet site
   - Sending info to other areas or managers
   - Newsletters
   - Idea forums
   - and other forms of communicating and sharing.

6. **Recognition and success is celebrated**
   - The best form of recognition is that the employee knows his/her idea was used.
   - Award a select parking spot for a week or month.
   - Post stickers in the work area with the idea and person's name.

- Top management tours the area and offers a personal "thank you," personal handwritten note – the more personal and sincere, the better.
- Idea metrics are monitored.

Idea Implementation Plan:

1. **Train and educate management and the design and implementation team.**

2. **Design the idea system/process:**
   - What the process will look like?
   - How will the expectations for ideas be communicated?
   - What resources will be needed to support?
   - How will employees be trained in the pilot areas?

3. **Pilot Program commences and learning takes place.**
   - Make the appropriate modifications and improvements based on what you learn. (PDCA).
   - Create experienced resources who can help with the broader effort later.
   - Determine implications for a broader effort.

4. **General training and broader launch.** Discuss what the appropriate timing is for the rollout plan.

CHAPTER SUMMARY – KAIZEN EVENTS AND DAILY KAIZEN: Kaizen Events and Daily Kaizen truly harvest the ideas of everyone and create the greatest continuous improvement leverage. Kaizen events are normal in Lean Government, yet they are viewed as a tool and the normal culture is not impacted. The goal is to embed Kaizen into the fabric of the way the organization does business.

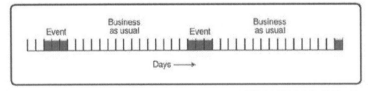

Kaizen Event or Business As Usual or Daily Practice?

www.shmula.com

RESOURCES:

[1]Robinson, Alan G. and Schroeder, Dean M. (2004). *Ideas are Free* and *The Idea-Driven Organization* (2014). Berrett-Koehler Publishers, Inc.

RESOURCE MATERIALS FOR IDEAS AND KAIZEN:

Akers, Paul (2012). *2 Second Lean – How to Grow People and Build a Fun Lean Culture*. Fast Cap Press. Imai, Masaaki (2012). *Gemba Kaizen: A Commonsense Approach to a Continuous Improvement Strategy, Second Edition*. McGraw Hill.

Chapter 12
Governance Structure

Ownership, accountability and responsibility

Having the necessary structural elements to support a sustainable Lean Government initiative is often overlooked. There is a rush to use Lean Government tools without a supporting infrastructure.

The questions that need to be initially asked:

Do you have a clear understanding of why you want to begin a Lean Government initiative?
> Why is now the right time?

Do you have the infrastructure to execute and track improvement activities?
> Do you have meaningful metrics?
> If not, are you prepared to establish infrastructure & metrics?

Can you really do "process improvement" on top of everything else you're doing?
> Are you "committed" or "supportive"?
> What are the recognition/consequences for subordinate staff?

Do you have a plan to engage the business community to gain their support?

Do you have a mechanism to incorporate the new skill sets and incentives into the expectations for your managers?
> Career paths, annual reviews, etc.?

Do you have qualified, reliable training/support partner?
> With significant public sector training/support experience?
> There is huge "partner" variation -- how will you choose?

Harvard's John Kotter advised not to start with a cultural thrust first. Lean Government is a "change initiative" comprised of the actions, behaviors (both covered in Chapter 2 – Leadership), and systems and structures (both covered in this chapter). A successful Lean Government structure is as follows (Figure 12.1). The roles and responsibilities details:

The Chief Executive (Governor, Agency Commissioner, County Manager, Mayor, City Manager, School Superintendent) responsibilities:

- Attend the entire initial Lean Government training for knowledge and demonstrated level of commitment.
- Attend Kaizen event report out sessions.
- Expect all of her/his direct reports to attend the initial training and attend Kaizen event report out sessions.
- Expect all of his/her direct reports (Executive Leadership Team) to "own" the Lean Government efforts in their respective areas of responsibility.
- Establish the following structural functions with the Lean Government Steering Committee:

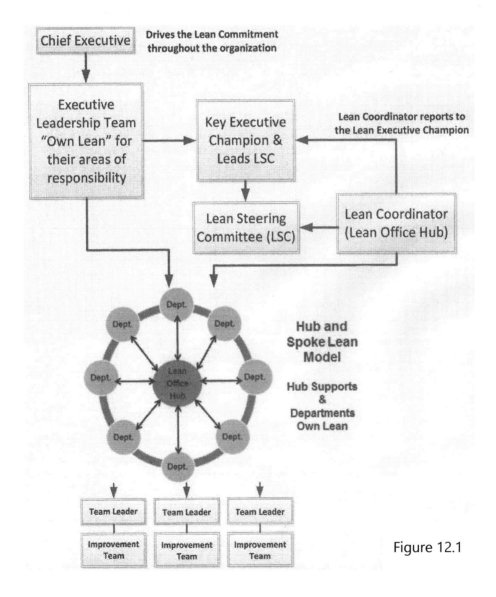

Figure 12.1

Executive Team Member responsibilities:

- Sets Lean Government expectations and ownership with their management team.
- Initiates efforts to identify all key processes, how they are doing, and identify improvement opportunities.
- Oversees the delivery of Lean Government introductory training (60-90 minutes) to their organization.
- Ensures all employees have a clear understanding of how to identify and remove wastes, how to identify and solve problems, and how to improve processes.
- Sponsors key Lean Government projects or oversees sponsors in her/his agency, department, or unit.
- Follows leader standard work and participates in Gemba walks to "see".

Executive Champion (an Executive team Member appointed by the Chief Executive to lead the Lean Government initiative and Lean Government Steering Committee meetings and actions) responsibilities**:**

- Reports directly to the Chief Executive and monitors Lean Government progress in the organization and intervenes, where necessary, on any issues requiring resolution that are brought to her/his attention. Is highly trusted and speaks for Lean Government on behalf of the Chief Executive.
- Lean Government Coordinator reports to and receives guidance from Executive Champion and seeks his/her support when obstacles arise.
- Coordinates efforts between departments, as necessary.

Lean Government Coordinator (or Lean Government Office Leader) responsibilities**:**

- Reports to the Executive Champion
- Well respected in the organization with high credibility and has sufficient "clout" with top management support and commitment
- Lean Government resource expertise for all areas to draw on and is the "Hub" for the Lean Government effort.
- Coordinates outside consulting resources and private sector partners
- Develops, modifies and coordinates all Lean Government training
- Monitors and tracks all Lean Government projects
- Communicates Lean Government progress to the organization via newsletters, intranet site, and other appropriate means.

Hub and Spoke Resource Support Model

Resources should be proficient in Lean and imbedded in each department reporting to the department head and reinforcing ownership for the department's Lean initiative – these are the "Spokes". The "Spokes" draw on the "Hub" resources as needed.

Lean Government Steering Committee (LSC) responsibilities – the key working oversight body for Lean Government governance:

Steering Committee Charter (suggested guidelines):

Purpose

The purpose of the Lean Government Steering Committee is to help guide the implementation of Lean Government to help achieve initiative goals. Specific goals of the LSC are:

- Introduce and/or expand the widespread use of organizational improvement methodologies found in the Lean Government approach; while embracing six sigma, change and quality management tools.
- Create a network of improvement 'experts' and practitioners across all departments to sustain the effort over time.
- Provide a forum for internal and external cooperation and support to help managers and department leaders fully utilize the tools and techniques available through these methodologies.

Scope

The LSC will oversee and provide input into the evolution and growth of the Lean Government within Government. Specifically, the LSC will:

- Create and implement a communication strategy
- Provide input into prioritization of major Lean Government projects (Kaizen events)
- Review and monitor project results
- Address obstacles to implementation
- Help establish longer term benchmarks and milestones for tracking implementation progress.
- Ensure financial tracking mechanisms are consistent
- Recognition of improvement successes

Membership - Size and Composition of the LSC

Membership is cross-functional with the Lean Government Executive Champion and the Lean Government Coordinator (or Lean Government office leader) being permanent members.

- Number of members can vary from 6-10.
- 3-4 members from the Executive Leadership Team.
- Membership term of 9-12 months, staggered, with new members coming on board.
- The Committee will be composed of representatives from the Departments.
- The Committee will be chaired by the Executive Champion.

Responsibilities of Membership

Members will make every effort to attend meetings as scheduled, and to follow-up on assignments or tasks that may result from Committee decisions. The Lean Government Coordinator will make every effort to schedule meetings to fit each member's calendar as is possible.

Meeting Frequency

It is expected that the Committee will meet approximately every month. The Lean Government Coordinator will be responsible for developing the meeting agenda with input from members and others, and circulating the agenda for review and comment prior to the meeting.

Decision-Making

Decisions of the Committee will be made by consensus (all members agree and support the decision). If consensus is not possible on a particular issue, decisions will be made by informed consent (all members can live with decision).

Relationships

The Committee and its members will seek out and actively work with others involved in continuous improvement efforts within the private sector, and other units of Government and education when it is anticipated that it will help support the achievement of Lean Government goals. The CI program operates under the umbrella of the .... Written progress reports and regular updates will be provided to the Sponsor, Steering Committee and Department Directors.

Lean Government Steering Committee Standard Work:

1. Agenda is issued one week in advance and copied via e-mail to all top managers, soliciting any inputs they have for the agenda.

2. LSC should be scheduled for 90 minutes (to allow enough time – can always adjourn early if the meeting is done) and be held once/month, without fail. Start on time.

3. Standing members of the LSC are the Lean Government Executive Champion and the Lean Government Coordinator.

4. LSC other members should rotate on and off every 9-12 months. The Chief Executive should approve the new members.

5. LSC minutes should be rotated each month among LSC members. Minutes should be published via e-mail to all top managers (to make sure they read them) and also posted on the Intranet shared site no later than one week after the meeting.

6. The next LSC meeting should be scheduled at the end of the current meeting (agenda item). Better yet, a 3-6 months future schedule is scheduled.

7. Standing agenda items:

   a. Review of previous minutes.

   b. Any additional items to be discussed.

   c. Update on Measure What matters status, including overall dashboard.

   d. Two managers to briefly (10 minutes max.) update their Lean Government activities, progress, and new identified opportunities for improvement.

   e. One Kaizen event process owner to update progress (10 minutes max.)

   f. Review of LSC checklists for Sustaining Change and Leadership (do once/6 months)

   g. Other agenda items.

   h. Setting the next SC meeting date and closure.

8. This Standard work should be reviewed by the Chief Executive with the LSC Chair a minimum of once/6 months to ensure compliance.

9. Audit ALL Standard Work compliance every six (6) months.

Process and Project Related Roles: most of the following roles are explained in Figures 12.2 and 12.3. A few roles will be covered after Figure 12.3 to provide more clarity.

Process Related Roles

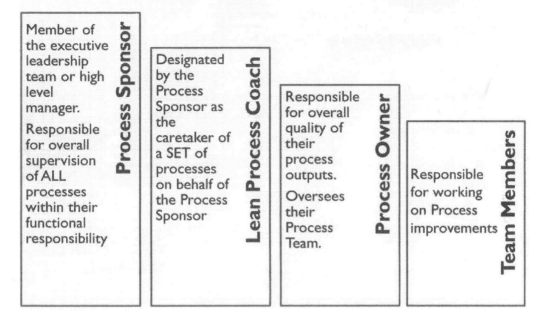

Figure 12.2

Project Related Roles

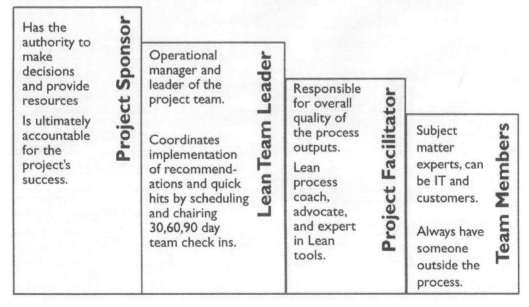

Figure 12.3

Project Sponsor/Champion Role:

- Drafts project charter and refines it with Team Leader
- Drafts preliminary Elevator Speech
- Approves the selection of team members and coordinates communications with team member supervisors and the team members in advance – no surprises
- Maintains knowledge and is informed as to project's progress
- Helps Team Leaders overcome roadblocks
- Facilitates the identification of resources for teams as needed
- Keeps Team Leaders focused on desired results
- If insurmountable events occur, redirects team focus and activities
- Keeps Executive Leader and Lean Government Executive Champion informed of project progress
- Approves rewards and recognition
- Disbands team upon completion of project or improvement

Team Members - considerations when selecting teams:

- Should number between 6 and 8 members for best results
- Should include opinion leaders
- Should represent organizational power equally
- Represents and considers diversity – high and low knowledge of the project
- Considers geography and co-locates (if possible)
- Must be supportive and exhibit a positive attitude
- Should be respected by co-workers
- Are able to efficiently arrange work

CHAPTER SUMMARY – GOVERNANCE – Key to a successful, sustainable, Lean Government initiative is to ensure this change is supported by the necessary structures and systems. The elements in this chapter support Chapter 3 on Change Management, especially the *WHY LEAN GOVERNMENT INITIATIVES FAIL* section near the end of Chapter 3.

REFERENCE MATERIALS FOR FURTHER READING:

Mann, David (2014). *Creating a Lean Government Culture: Tools to Sustain Lean Conversions, Third Edition.* CRC Press, Taylor & Francis Group, LLC.

Chapter 13

Strategic Lean Government
Lean Management System – Lean Strategic Thinking

While the end of Chapter 3 covered the reasons Lean fails, this chapter expands on what can be done to create sustainable success that is embedded in the culture of the organization. We will cover the broader approach to a Lean Strategy that can become the organizational DNA. To date, examples of sustainable, successful strategic Lean initiatives are rare. If they do become reality, they can be undone by new management that doesn't understand what Lean really entails. Tools implementations are the usual norm, but by only implementing Lean tools, huge opportunities are lost. Leadership that is steeped in Lean thinking is required to move to this strategic level.

This chapter is intended to provide an overview of Lean Government as a strategy for the organization. More in-depth resources can be explored further.

TRUE NORTH (Figure 13.1): **Leaders must convey a compelling vision to the organization.** True North is the strategic forward direction for the organization as illustrated in this graphic:

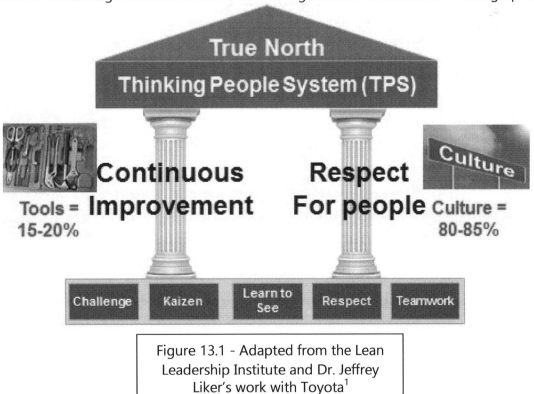

Figure 13.1 - Adapted from the Lean Leadership Institute and Dr. Jeffrey Liker's work with Toyota[1]

Challenge means to set a stretch target – It can be based on a critical customer need, level of urgency to address, financial leverage that's created, etc. A challenge causes people to have passion to meet and succeed in the challenge which, in turn, leads to greater learning, accomplishments and successful improvements. If we don't know what the goal is, how will we know when we get there?

- You first have to know how you're doing in data terms. As previously noted, the question in Government "How are you doing" is often met with "We don't know". For example, let's say it takes 58 days to process a license application.
- Once the current state baseline in known, then the future state target must be established. If the target was 56 days, then the organization would tend to just try and work harder with the same methods and approaches.
- Establishing a minimum 50% improvement goal in 29 days becomes a challenge (and it might even be 20 or 10 days). Once this is done, the old ways and paradigms of doing things are not equipped to meet the challenge goal. This drives the need to apply new thinking and approaches to creatively bridge the gap and meet the challenge. People generally respond well to a challenge as it energizes them to seek out new ways to get there. The old paradigm of "the way we do things around here" is broken.
- Utilizing Lean techniques facilitates the ability to meet challenge goals.

Kaizen is continuous improvement throughout the organization, not just a series of 3-5 day "events" (which is the model most organizations follow). More in depth details are covered on Kaizen in Chapter 11.

"Learn to See" means always going to where the work is done (the "Gemba") and understanding all the aspects of the work. Managers never have the time to truly see how the current state processes perform. They are consumed by the "here and now" day-to-day activities of their own jobs. Normally, when the need arises, they need to go "troubleshoot" a problem and what has gone astray in the process, and, once "solved", they immediately remove themselves from the process details and return to their "regular work".

An action item for all leaders (a "leader" is anyone who has associates working for them – a broader definition than just top management) is to take a full eight-hour day, pick a process that is in significant need of improvement and spend the full day only "seeing" what happens in the process from the beginning to the end (or get as far as able in one day). Make sure there are no interruptions and that everyone understands what the leader is doing. It isn't to find fault with the people; it's to find out what's wrong with the process. Amazing things are discovered, including:

- Associates' ideas and frustrations come to the surface:
  o How to correct errors and rework
  o How to consolidate process steps or forms, or even consolidate or eliminate them
- Unnecessary steps are being done

- Directions about eliminated steps were never passed on to others and the steps are still being done
- Training materials are partial, poor or non-existent
- Duplication, fragmentation and overlap in the process
- Misinterpretation of current statutes and ordinances
- And many other discoveries

Respect and Teamwork focus on the most important resources – people. Leadership, change management and governance are also linked with a key resource – employees. Employees must be trained to identify wastes (Chapter 6) and develop problem-solving skills (Chapter 7). As seen in Figure 13.1, the Lean tools and techniques are estimated at 15-20%, while the organizational culture (actions, behaviors, systems and structures) is 80-85% of the process in order for a true Lean management system to develop and flourish.

Leadership must be Lean-proficient and hands-on, not isolated in an office with an occasional trip to a conference room. Leaders must participate in Gemba walks with a purpose in mind, not just randomly walking around to talk to employees. The Gemba walk must focus on reinforcing the True North principles and openly listening and soliciting input from everyone. Leaders should also be good coaches and not tell everyone what to do or solve problems on the spot without knowing the real problem.

Developing a true culture of respect and teamwork for everyone is hard work. The following is a leadership sequence which grows Lean leaders, and subsequently a Lean culture (figure 13.2):

Figure 13.2[1]

THE SHINGO MODEL FOR OPERATIONAL EXCELLENCE[2]

Combining the True North compass above with the Shingo Criteria (Figures 13.3 and 13.4) creates a comprehensive approach to developing a true Lean Management System and organizational culture.

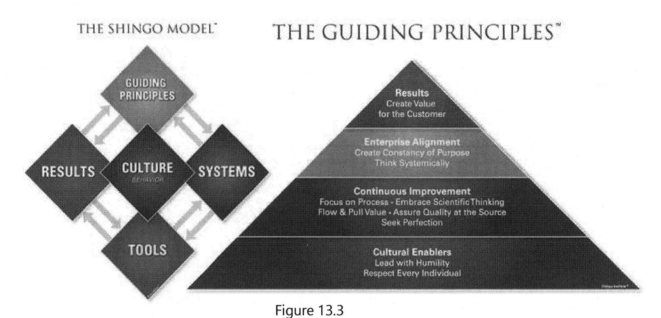

Figure 13.3

Shingo Core	Guiding Principles	Supporting Principles	QPIC Alignment
Cultural Enablers	Lead with Humility Respect Every Individual	Nurture Long-term Relationships Empower and Involve Everyone Develop People Assure a Safe Environment	LLD for all Leaders: surveys, 360⁰ feedback and development plans Lean Coaching & Supervisory Training (Toyota Kata) Lean Steering Committee (LSC) Change Management Principles PDCA and 7 Wastes training for everyone.

Figure 13.4

Continuous Process Improvement	Focus on Process Embrace Scientific Thinking Flow & Pull Value Assure Quality at the Source Seek Perfection	Stabilize Processes Rely on Data Standardize Processes Insist on Direct Observation Focus on Value Stream Keep it Simple & Visual Identify & Eliminate Waste Integrate Improvement with Work	Lean and Six Sigma Toolkit: the 7 Wastes, Value Stream Mapping, Project Charters, Stakeholder Analysis, 5S, Visual Controls, Standard Work, Dynamic Data Collection tools, Mistake-Proofing, Action Plans, "One stop shopping" increasing Flow, PDCA, TOC, TWI, etc. "Learn to See" "Right the 1st Time" and Reduce Variation
Enterprise Alignment	Create Constancy of Purpose Think Systemically	See Reality Focus on Long Term Align Systems Align Strategy	Vision, Mission, Principles and cascading Goals into a cohesive MWM Balanced Scorecard and Accountability Map. Cascading improvement tracking. Clear ownership alignment. Hoshin Kanri Performance appraisals linked.

Figure 13.4

| Results | Create Value for the Customer | Measure What Matters

Align Behaviors with Performance

Identify Cause & Effect Relationships | Measure What Matters (MWM)

Voice of the Customer methods

DIG (Dynamic Idea Generation) – Daily Kaizen

Dynamic Data Generation

LSC tracks progress.

Monthly reporting of improvements and savings via Finance. |

Figure 13.4

LEAN MANAGEMENT IMPLEMENTATION MODEL

There are a variety of models that can be utilized to move from a tools and techniques implementation to a comprehensive Lean Management System (LMS) implementation.

The figure below (Figure 13.5) starts with a "demonstration phase" where top management is provided the initial Lean training and experience in an interactive two- day workshop which works on some of the current state process problems. This provides the opportunity for top management to learn and understand what Lean is all about and then decide "what comes next".

Figure 13.5

We believe that this is an excellent model for the following reasons:
- Lean Government education starts with top management – understanding the tools and techniques along with how to begin a Lean Government initiative
- Several Kaizen events to demonstrate success
- Kick off Lean activities in multiple departments to gain some experience

HOSHIN KANRI

The terminology evolved in Japan, with the Bridgestone Tire Company being credited with coining the name Hoshin Kanri in 1965. The best translation is the *management of the strategic direction setting process in the organization.* Terms that are often used include: Hoshin Planning, Strategy Deployment and Policy Deployment. While there are many resources that provide more detailed information on Hoshin Kanri (several of which are listed at the end of this chapter), this book provides an overview.

Hoshin is a broad strategic view of the organization and the forwards plans. The most common form is known as the Hoshin Planning X matrix[2] (Figure 13.6) :

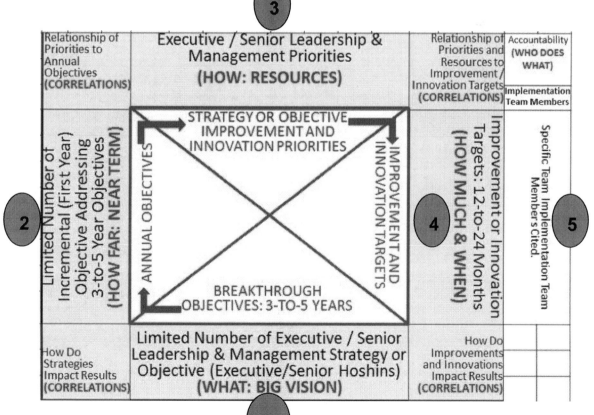

Figure 13.6[2]

1. Big Vision – This area is driven by the Vision-Mission-Principles of the organizational strategy and is long term in nature. There could be 5-7 key objectives that are listed here, with the supporting specific long-term breakthrough objectives For example in a city:
   a. Citizen Safety
   b. Thriving Economy
   c. Financial Strength
   d. Clean and Healthy Environment
   e. Excellent Education System
2. Near Term Goals – This area targets the annual specific goals or objectives that support the Big Vision.
3. Resources – These are the resources that will need to be deployed to address the specific key projects that will support the strategy and metrics. This addresses more of the implementation.
4. Improvement Targets – These are the bigger strategic improvements.
5. Team Members – Determine who specifically is responsible for implementing the tactics and projects.

The Hoshin Kanri Planning X-Matrix would then be filled in with the inter-relationships between each of the sections.

Arizona State example of a Lean Government strategic approach:

Arizona launched its statewide Lean Government effort in earnest in early 2016. Governor Doug Ducey, formerly CEO of Cold Stone Creamery, was a Lean Government advocate when he took office in 2015.

Two visuals (Figures 13.7 & 13.8) demonstrate how Arizona State Government has embraced a Lean strategy.

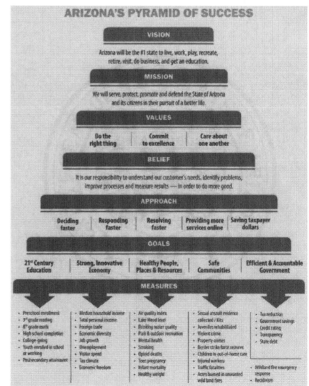

Figure 13.7

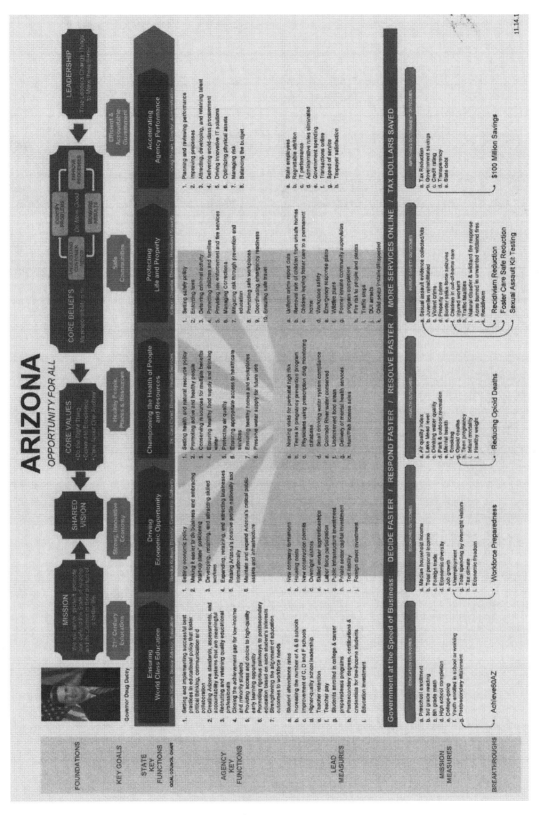

Figure 13.8

Both figures illustrate a cascading approach to developing a comprehensive, cascading set of Vision-Mission-Principles/Values-Key Goals-Functions-Measures with corresponding defined ownership. This approach is strategic in nature and provides understanding and guidance to everyone on the direction in which the state is moving.

CHAPTER SUMMARY: The intent of this chapter was to provide an overview and some insight into the various strategic approaches to Lean Government. The key takeaway is that the vast majority of Lean efforts do not get this far and stop at the tools and techniques phase, minimizing the true potential for Lean Government. Key cascading metrics (Key Process Indicators [KPIs] and/or Measure What Matters [MWM]) coupled with well-defined process owners drive accountability and results and need to be in place in order to have a truly successful Lean Government.

REFERENCES:

[1]Liker, Jeffrey K. and Trachilis, George. Lean Leadership Institute. https://leanleadership.guru/
[2]Shingo Award for Operational Excellence. http://www.shingoprize.org/
[3]Watson, G.H. (2003), *"Policy Deployment: Consensus Method of Strategy Realization,"* Quality into the 21st Century: Perspectives on Quality and Competitiveness for Sustained Performance, pp. 191-218, T. Conti, Y. Kondo, and G.H. Watson (Eds.), ASQ Quality Press.
[4]Anderson, Randy K. (2015). *The Basics of Hoshin Kanri*. CRC Press.

REFERENCE MATERIALS FOR FURTHER READING ON LEAN STRATEGY:

Balle, Michael; Jones, Daniel; Chaize, Jacques; and Fiume, Orest (2017). *The Lean Strategy: Using Lean to Create Competitive Advantage, Unleash Innovation, and Deliver Sustainable Growth,* McGraw-Hill.

Chapter 14
Lean Government ROI

How do we know Lean is worth doing?

It is important to remember that Lean is based on an organization that is continually focused on:
- Teaching all employees to identify and remove wastes and identify and solve problems which can also leverage process improvements.
- Leaders/managers/supervisors, at every level, are focused on their key role as a coach for their employees.

Any job reductions should only be done via attrition. As Lean continues to gain momentum in Government, a key question arises:

"Are we really saving any money (what is the Return on Investment [ROI])?"

Where to Start?

Lean improvement efforts should be based on having a good foundation in Lean principles and techniques training, coupled with good facilitation and coaching to develop Lean internal resources. This doesn't happen with one course or Kaizen event; it takes deliberate practice.

A good place to start is to understand the key value streams within the organization. A value stream includes the start to the end of a key business process, including all the value added and non-value added activities and actions that are provided in a product or service that the customer cares about. Some examples are:

- Finance – A/P, A/R, Payroll, Capital Project Management, revenue management
- Business development – licensing, permitting, building inspections, business retention, business recruitment
- Engineering – approval cycles, review processes
- Procurement – POs, master agreements, general procurement practices
- Police – false alarms, deployment strategies, dispatch centers, response times, crime rates/categories, evidence rooms
- Fire – false alarms, prevention strategies, EMS calls, fire inspections
- Utilities – water, sewer, gas, electric
- Public Works – maintenance, vehicle uptime, work order management, snow plowing, improved safety, PM program, 5S
- Parks and Recreation – summer deployments, pools, park maintenance
- HR – hiring process, on-boarding, benefits, off-boarding

As an example of value stream, let's look at the Department of Public Works in a city and the process of maintaining city streets. Many aspects go into this process, including asking the following:

- How are requests for street repairs generated?
- Is there a preventative maintenance program?
- How are work assignments given?
- How long does it take to complete the repairs?
- What is the cost of making the repairs?
- How are the vehicles and paving equipment serviced and maintained?
- How the customer is notified when the repairs will be done and when they are completed?

Methods of Making Process Improvements
There are numerous approaches to make tangible gains:

Developing Preliminary Data Collection and Process Metrics – This is relatively easy to do and can be implemented immediately within a work group. When the question is asked "How are you doing," the dominant answer is "We don't know." It's hard to make a 50% reduction in the time it takes to start and issue a business license if you don't know how many days it currently takes.

1. **Errors and Rework** – The same lack of information holds true when it comes to understanding the error and/or rework rate in a process. Having the people actually working in the process use simple data collection techniques, such as checklists and concentration diagrams, can lead to major "ah-ha" discoveries and, therefore, fairly quick fixes. This was covered in Chapter 7 on Problem Solving.

2. **Benchmarking** – Chapter 5 on Benchmarking covered the concepts and approach to take, along with some examples.

3. **Laws, Statutes, and Ordinances** – Significant instances have occurred where these have been established to address a problem without truly understanding what the real problem is.

   Examples of eliminating wastes in this area can be found in Arizona, Colorado, and Rhode Island, where state agencies are addressing current legal mandates and determining which ones need to be rescinded, combined or rewritten. This has been especially beneficial on mandates related to making it difficult to establish a business, since making changes in this area can yield high economic benefits.

4. **Organizational Discipline** – This category is based on:
a. Policies, procedures and well-documented processes are already in place; however, the organization just doesn't have the discipline to follow and do what is supposed to be done.

This doesn't require a focused improvement effort to reinvent things – just do or follow what is already in place.

b. Accessibility to the appropriate information – High levels of waste are associated with the right information not being able to be accessed by the individuals who need it. Much of this falls on how documentation is generated and accessed, usually leading to a critical review of the organization's Internet and Intranet sites, coupled with training and good visual controls.

5. **What is the Customer Experience?** – As covered in Chapter 4 on Customers, a pure review of how easy is it for the customer to access the information can yield good gains. The need is to truly "walk in the customer's shoes" to increase the ability for the customer to submit information to be "right the first time." Is the Government web site easy to understand and navigate for customers? Does it contain too many words or pages or is it built more on simple-to-follow checklists with visual examples? Where are the errors and rework occurring from the customer input and information that is received?

6. **Employee Ideas** – Employees have the ability to identify Lean ideas that can create incremental gains by improving services and/or reducing wastes. The target for organizations doing this well is a minimum of one implemented idea per month per employee (some organizations are well beyond this). This can't be done in a haphazard way, as any new ideas must have team acceptance and must be built into the standard work training instructions to ensure process consistency. This is not a traditional suggestion and was covered in Chapter 11 (Daily Kaizen).

7. **Rapid Improvement Events (RIEs), also known as Kaizen events**

Many Government Lean efforts are focused on doing RIEs with the misconception that this is what Lean is all about. RIEs are full-time, consecutive-day events (usually no more than five days, though there could be fewer days, based on the event scope). An event team (usually no more than 10 members) is made up of individuals who work in the value stream that is the focus of the RIE, along with other individuals who don't work in the value stream, service providers, customers, etc. The makeup of each event team is determined based on the scope and need.

Since Kaizen events are very intensive, they also have the associated costs of facilitators and consultants, wages and benefits of all attendees and preparation work that is done before the event. This creates the critical need to ensure the event has been chosen wisely. It's very important that there is an excellent ROI related to Kaizen events. The team would be very disappointed if the savings in time and costs were insignificant, not to mention how that would be negatively communicated throughout the organization.

It should be a high impact value stream – create a prioritization selection grid – Select the best candidate from among the Project Charter candidates (see Chapter 10 – Project Charters and

Project Selection). That allows for greater opportunity for savings in general and an increased probability of tangible, quantifiable savings that can be identified as a return on the investment of the Kaizen event. A prioritization table should be constructed based on the appropriate project rating criteria.

SO, WHAT IS THE RETURN ON INVESTMENT (ROI)?

First, it's critical to have one person or a small group, preferably in the Finance function, to consistently determine all ROI calculations. It makes the numbers credible to the organization and eliminates huge swings in calculated returns or savings.

THE INVESTMENT part is relatively easy to calculate including employee wages and benefits associated with the time devoted to the improvement activity, outside consulting costs, any supplies or materials and acquisition costs (office equipment, desks, software, etc.).

THE RETURN part is where the real work needs to be done. Returns may come in many different forms. Following are only some examples:

- **Soft savings** are based more on such things as productivity gains or new services that are provided. They are considered soft in that the overall employee cost totals did not go down. For example, one person was freed up from doing wasteful activities and was re-deployed in another process area.

- **Hard savings** come from reducing the real costs of goods or services. This would include any employee attrition (overall employee cost totals did go down), reduction in outside vendor costs and elimination of wastes. Increased revenues are clear based on established baselines.

THE FOLLOWING ARE AREAS FOR ROI CALCULATIONS:

1. Employee costs:
   a. **Attrition** – This results when employees leave the organization through retirement or move to another location and they don't have to be replaced due to increased efficiencies. This is a hard cost savings and represents the total employee costs of a full time equivalent (FTE) person, including wages and benefits. Lean process improvements should never be the cause of layoffs.

   b. **Cost avoidance** – Lean gains eliminate the need to add individuals and/or result in cancelled open requisitions. This still becomes an FTE calculation of what are costs were avoided.

c. **Enhanced call centers and Internet sites** – The City of Denver, for example, has calculated that it costs $3.11 to pick up and answer each phone call. By enhancing websites and the customer information experience, the city can measure the call volume going down and the website "click rate" going up. Fewer calls X $3.11 per call = savings.

d. **Greater consistency in how work is done**. This should be coupled with reduced variation through better training and Standard Work. For example, if there was less variation in Medicaid social worker assessments, the cost variation would be reduced and the overall costs could be reduced – these would be hard, quantifiable dollars based on reduced contracted outside service costs.

e. **Fewer errors and less rework** – Understanding problems and root causes leads to solutions which drive better, faster and less expensive services. Error and rework data is usually unknown when a project is proposed.

2. **Acquisition cost avoidance** -Eliminate the need for any new acquisitions, such as equipment, vehicles, office equipment and software. This includes finding things that were thought to be lost or stolen as well as repurposing freed up assets. These would be hard costs that could be calculated.

3. **Providing enhanced or additional services:**
   a. This would include processes such as faster permitting and licensing. This could be measured by the number of licenses issued per employee per month, before and after. Some of the revenue returns here would be in the areas of:
      - Faster, increased business acquisition, drawing more businesses to locate in the area, thereby generating more taxes, increased local spending and hiring of more employees.
      - Faster building licenses = construction = revenues
   b. Increase revenues by collecting delinquencies faster at a higher percentage rate.
   c. Reduce police and fire false alarms – Municipalities have calculated the costs associated with false alarms. Redeploying police and fire coverage and base site station locations could allow municipalities to refocus on reducing crime and fire or property damage rates.
   d. Lean improvements result in better flow, office design and logistics. These would be both hard and soft cost savings based on greater productivity

4. **Greater employee satisfaction** can be measured based on turnover rates and turnover root causes.
   a. Greater employee retention and less recruitment costs lead to savings in advertising costs and agency fees as well as less managerial time spent on recruiting and interviewing.

   b. Less absenteeism and overtime costs.

   c. Enhanced safety performance, which results in less worker's compensation costs and reduced overtime costs.

   d. Better cross-trained employees means less overtime requirements, since multiple employees can do the same function.

5. Procurement:

   a. More time to take vendor discount terms – money saved.

   b. More time for better negotiations – money saved.

   c. More time for better RFQ/RFP documentation - better bids to better meet the needs.

   d. Explore vendor inventory, consignment and on-site stocking options.

   e. More time for many other avenues for savings and better vendor service.

6. Greater customer/taxpayer satisfaction:

   a. Citizens want to move to the area, resulting in increases in the number of residents, services and housing.

   b. Fewer complaints to be answered.

   c. There is less need to respond to Freedom of Information Act (FOIA) requests.

7. Reduced litigation and adjudication costs:

   a. Processing litigations more quickly leads to quicker case resolutions and revenues.

   b. Better processes lead to litigation avoidance, although a baseline would first need to be established in order to determine this.

8. Other areas will vary by department, agency, city, county and school.

Chapter 15
Software Development

Blending Agile and Lean Thinking for More Efficient IT Development[1]

If you automate a junk process, you get automated junk.

Governments' information technology (IT) projects don't always deliver the promised results. Combine performance problems with a reputation for being late and over budget and it's easy to see why officials are often reluctant to take on major IT initiatives. The problem isn't inherent in Government projects, however; it's caused by the traditional "waterfall" approach (see below) to project planning. And it can be averted by using a different kind of project planning, a Lean approach known as "Agile" development. Agile development and Lean management can lead to more cost-effective, timely production of information technology that better meets users' needs. One of the first steps is to create a value added process and PDCA it. After this is done, it is then time to provide the IT solution.

Traditional Waterfall Development
Waterfall development has been the dominant approach among IT professionals for years. This approach is about trying to understand the customer's new needs and then working on the development for months, after which the final output is released – a top-to-bottom process. Customer feedback is given when the overall project is completed.

One study indicates that 45 percent of the features in a typical system are never used, and only 13 percent are always used (Figure 15.1). Overall, success rates for IT development, based on a sampling of multiple publications and studies, are not good:
- Approximately 31 percent of projects get cancelled.
- Approximately 66 percent of projects don't meet customer needs and are, therefore, considered failures.
- More than 50 percent of projects exceed their budgets by 200 percent.
- Deliverables are not well planned or well managed.
- Project managers could use more training.
- Approximately 10 percent of the developed code was actually used.
- Approximately 82 percent of projects cite waterfall practices as the primary reason for failure.

Figure 15.1: The Features and Functions that Are Actually Used in a Typical System:

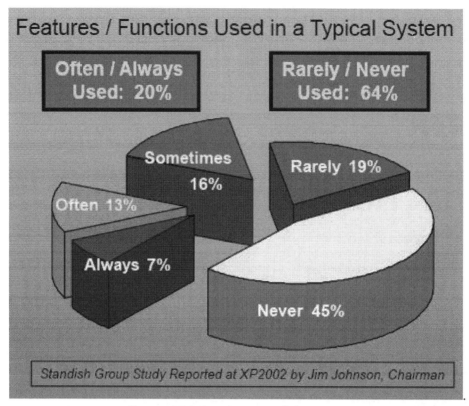

Figure 15.1 Source: Standish Group

Many articles have been written about chaos theory (expect the unexpected, things that are effectively impossible to predict or control) and how it relates to waterfall software development. This is because so many uncertainties and variables can come into play when software is developed. Also, some of the assumptions waterfall development makes are unrealistic, such as the idea that customer needs are clearly defined upon going into the project, the needs of the client department are thoroughly vetted and agreed upon, and the requirements can be accurately determined at the beginning of the project. Waterfall moves along a straight path, based on initial inputs and assumptions, so errors or miscalculations made at the outset of the project will be included in the final product. Waterfall also assumes that timeframes and budgets are easy to predict in the beginning; many waterfall developments fall in quarterly timeframes for progress and outputs, which is not nearly the frequency needed for reviewing progress and alignment with customer needs, and soliciting customer feedback (which is the final step in a waterfall process, after the project is completed).

The Evolution of Agile
In 2001, a group of 17 IT professional gathered to develop an alternative to the waterfall approach, which they called "Agile."[1] The group agreed to an "Agile Manifesto" (see Figure 15.2)[2], which included several values aimed at making IT development more effective:
1. Individuals and interactions should take precedence over processes and tools.

2. Working software is the desired output, as opposed to comprehensive documentation.
3. Customer collaboration is superior to negotiating contracts with clients.
4. Responding to change is more important than blindly following a plan.

1. The highest priority should be satisfying the customer through early and continuous delivery of valuable software.
2. Changing requirements should be welcomed, even late in development. Agile processes harness change for the customer's competitive advantage.
3. Working software should be delivered as frequently as possible.
4. Business people and developers need to work together every day, throughout the project.
5. Projects should be built around motivated individuals. Give them the environment and support they need, and trust them to get the job done.
6. The most efficient and effective method of conveying information to and within a development team is face-to-face conversation.
7. Working software is the primary measure of progress.
8. Agile processes promote sustainable development. The sponsors, developers, and users should be able to maintain a constant pace indefinitely.
9. Continuous attention to technical excellence and good design enhances agility.
10. Simplicity – the art of maximizing the amount of work not done – is essential.
11. The best architectures, requirements, and designs emerge from self-organizing teams.
12. The team needs to reflect on how to become more effective at regular intervals, and then tune and adjust its behavior accordingly.

Figure 15.2: The Principles of the Agile Manifesto

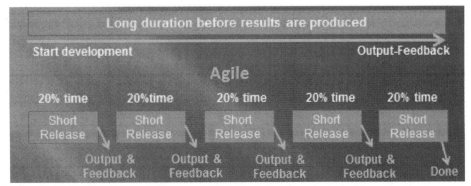

Figure 15.3: Differences between a Waterfall Approach and an Agile Approach
Waterfall = Entire Timeframe

Agile Provides (Figure 15.3):

Decreased Risk	More Feedback Points
More Feedback	More Time with Clients
Less Confusion	Less Time Needed Before Adjustments
Greater Employee Satisfaction	or Corrections are Made

The group developed the following key aspects of the system and terminology concepts (Figure 15.4):

1. The overall software client needs would be broken down to segments (known as stories) that are prioritized by their importance for development; this is known as backlog grooming. The team would do this based on the customer's prioritized needs.

2. Stories (a segment or element the backlog development needs) would then be developed. The suggested story structure is: "As a <user type> I want to <do some action> so that <desired result>." This helps so the development team can identify the user, action and required result in a request, and it is a simple way of writing requests that anyone can understand (e.g., "As a user I want a tool bar on the screen so that I can easily drop in changes").

3. The prioritized sections would be broken into smaller sections, or stories, lasting 1-4 weeks; these are called sprints, and each sprint ends with a working functional product for customer review. Each sprint team, normally of six to 10 people, would be dedicated full time. (There could be more team members, based on the complexity of the software development, but smaller teams generally work better.) Ideally, all team members should be at the same site for ease of communication and coordination.

4. A sprint planning meeting is then held with the assigned sprint team to determine what details are required to perform the work for the current sprint. This includes developing a detailed plan with elements and timeframes. Various techniques such as Planning Poker[3], can be used to determine a consensus for the team time requirements.

5. The sprint is then broken down to daily assignments for each team member. Each sprint should include a daily review of progress, called a scrum, for approximately 15 minutes at the beginning of each day to review what was completed the day before, what the team expects to complete on the current day, and any impediments team members may have experienced.

6. At the end of each sprint, the customer would review the functional output and review the prioritized product backlog. The backlog priorities could change based on the output of each sprint.

7. The team leader, or scrum master, monitors project progress, provides support to the team, and helps remove obstacles that team members may be experiencing.

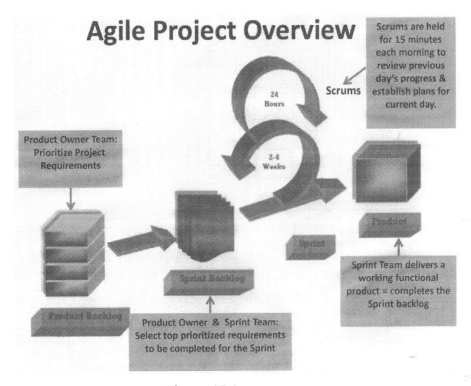

Figure 15.4

Integrating Lean with Agile

Agile is clearly aligned with the core Lean principles:

1. Adding value for the customer
2. Mapping value streams
3. Creating flow
4. Keeping pace with the customer demand rate
5. Getting it right the first time, thereby eliminating errors and rework

Adding Value for the Customer. This is all about clearly understanding what the customer wants to change, fix, improve or enhance. Any IT development project should ensure that the customer has a clear, comprehensive understanding of what they want to do and the desired outcomes. It's not enough for a customer to describe the desired outcomes; the customer's team or department also needs to be completely on-board with those outcomes. Many times, this is not the case. More time should be spent on the front end of any IT software development to clearly specify what outcomes are required and to make sure that everyone involved has the same clear understanding of all the appropriate operational definitions.

Agile offers an advantage for customer deliverables that are not well defined because these issues will be discovered much earlier in the software development process. Because Agile breaks down the project development into key stories that are then prioritized, customer communication is significantly better than in a traditional waterfall process. Within two to four weeks, Agile will produce the first demonstration deliverable for the customer to evaluate; along with the opportunity to look at the remaining stories and priorities in the backlog that still need to be developed.

A **Project Charter** document can be adapted to support the Agile process (see Figure 15.5). The customer fills out the project charter and delivers it to the Agile team, providing a good process for clarifying and verifying any changes that need to be made.

Project Name:			Location:		
Business Case:			Problem Statement:		
Project Scope:	IN		Goal:		
			Expected Direct Benefits:		Target
	OUT		Expected Indirect Benefits:		Target
Agile Team					
Scrum Master:					
Member			Total Benefits:		
Member					
Member			SPECIAL NOTES:		
Member					
Member					
Member					
Member					

Figure 15.5

Mapping Key Value Systems, or Learning to See. Too many projects are initiated without a clear understanding of how the current process operates, including all of the process wastes and inefficiencies. Nothing should be automated until the current process has gone through a Lean management process to remove wastes; automating a junk process provides automated junk. Understanding the process and its outcomes happens in the actual work area, where "the action is," and not with a few high level managers having a discussion in a conference room. When managers take the time to go to the work area and understand in great detail what actually happens, they "learn to see," which includes being amazed at how things are really done, including the amount of variation.

Creating Flow. A process should be designed with as few handoffs as possible before the software is created. Employees often say "we have to do it this way," but don't just accept that assertion; look for the facts that support it and make sure that any existing legislation or mandates are truly valid. Tribal knowledge, along with how effectively or ineffectively training is transmitted over time, creates beliefs about why "we have to do it this way" that usually aren't true.

The first step in getting past these beliefs is to clearly understand the current state of how things are actually done in as much detail as possible. Then, examine the current state for wastes such as errors and rework, and ask workers about their areas of frustration and any ideas they may have to improve the process. This information allows the organization to design a streamlined and effective "future state". This future state design should be tested using the iterative "Plan-Do-Check-Act/Adjust" cycle. Once these steps have been taken, an Agile development process can begin.

Keeping Pace with the Customer Demand Rate, or Pulling from the Customer. Agile is aligned with customer needs by creating useable output than can be demonstrated and tested in much shorter cycle times than waiting many months for a waterfall software output that might have missed the customer's mark.

Getting It Right the First Time. Each step of the development is tested to ensure that what is being designed is what the customer needs. Looking at the current state error and rework rates allows Agile developers to take corrective actions and mistake-proof the new software.

CHAPTER SUMMARY – LEAN SOFTWARE DEVELOPMENT

Why, then, isn't Agile used more often? People, and organizations, are resistant to change. In a magazine article, Steve Denning[4] cited a number of perceived objections to Agile. They include the idea that Agile is only for stars, that it doesn't fit in the organizational culture, that it only works for small projects, that it requires coworkers to be all in one place, that it lacks project management processes, and that it is just a fad. None of these points are really impediments to using Agile.

Agile is a Leaner approach to developing software than the traditional waterfall approach, creating more feedback and, thus, better alignment with the customer's needs. For the same reasons, Agile decreases risk and creates less confusion and greater employee satisfaction. With Agile, organizations use much less resource time discovering the need for corrections or adjustments.

Agile helps organizations deliver better and more successful projects, faster, and at lower costs. There are challenges, of course. Leaders and management need to have a clearer understanding of what Agile is, what it does, and its associated benefits than most currently do. Agile is also more successful with a greater level of communication from leaders and management. It also creates a greater need for customer interface and feedback loops. But there is really no reason not to explore and embrace Agile for software development. With proper guidance and management support, the risks are extremely low, and the benefits are great.

REFERENCES:

[1]Kenworthy, Harry. (April 2014). *Blending Agile and Lean Thinking for More Efficient IT Development*, pages 66-71. Government Finance Review Magazine.

[2]See the "*Manifesto for Agile Software Development*" at http://Agilemanifesto.org/.

[3]Planning Poker is available at no charge from sources such as MountainGoatSoftware.com.

[4]Denning, Steve. (April 17, 2012). *"The Case Against Agile: Ten Perennial Management Objections"*. Forbes Magazine.

Chapter 16

Lean Government General Principles and Examples

Overarching: Develop Measures What Matter: Cascaded from Vision-Mission-Outcomes = Key Goals/Metrics with Process Ownership = Accountability Maps

LEAN GOVERNMENT GENERAL PRINCIPLES

1. Focus on areas with high leverage and set Challenge Improvement Goals/Targets (at least 50% improvements).

2. One Stop Shopping whenever and wherever possible – the customer only has to see one person to complete their business.

3. Right the first time – identify and eliminate all sources of errors and rework – this is huge.

4. Understand customer needs and reduce waste for the customer:

   a. Easy forms
   b. Easy websites to navigate
   c. Identify info they need and make it easy to get
   d. High use of checklists

5. Really "Learn to See" the wastes in all processes by going to the actual work area.

6. Benchmark ("steal shamelessly and legally") from others to start at in an improved current state and then create an improved future state.

7. Ensure statutes/ordinances/laws are really being adhered to and have not morphed over time into unintended consequences. Get rid of the old stuff that isn't necessary and leads to waste and unnecessary costs.

8. Engage everyone in Daily Kaizen = Dynamic Daily Data Collection and Idea Generation. This becomes the culture.

9. A leader is anyone who has people working for them. Hire great people and teach them how to be great coaches.

10. 5S – Organize the workplace so any items necessary to do work can be found within 60 seconds.

SOME CITY/COUNTY LEAN PROJECT EXAMPLES

1. Finance:

   a. Accounts Payable Cycle Time Reduction
   b. Tax Collection Cycle Time to Deposit – reduce time to deposit
   c. Property Assessment Process – reduce time
   d. Payroll Process – reduce time and improve accuracy
   e. Invoices and Taxation – reduce process cycle times
   f. Accounts Payable process - improve process to achieve 100% of available discounts
   g. AP sources of errors or rework –Concentration Diagrams and Check Sheets
   h. Improve interdepartmental deposit process
   i. Review viability of warehouse to improve pricing to other departments and windshield time for field personnel
   j. RFQ/RFP Process
   k. Capital assets accurate inventory tracking
   l. Improve the capital project management process

2. Information Technology (IT)

   a. Lean out processes before IT automates
   b. Enhanced employee directories for communications
   c. Filing and e-mail protocols and naming structures
   d. Help desk functions
   e. 5S on electronic files

3. Purchasing and Procurement:

   a. Purchase Order cycle time reduction
   b. 5S and Visual
   c. P-Card usage
   d. Blanket and catalog procurement processes
   e. Streamlining RFP/RFQ processes
   f. Capital project spending – Lean construction

4. Fleet:

   a. Shop organization – Parts and tools inventory storage and retrieval
   b. Training assessment
   c. Consolidation of vehicle types
   d. Vehicle Preventative Maintenance and reducing vehicle downtimes
   e. Standard work for equipment maintenance
   f. 5S the facility and all vehicles for standardization
   g. Insurance claims processing
   h. Accident analysis and reduction

5. Departments. of Public Works and/or Water Department:

   a. Reduce time delays in the field
   b. Work order request and deployment
   c. Work order complaint analysis
   d. Standardization of trucks and work procedures
   e. Street repairs – time to fix potholes
   f. Garbage removal and street cleanliness
   g. Fleet Management, including 5S maintenance facility
   h. Safety – reduction in accident rates
   i. Vendor hardware inventory maintenance
   j. Snowplow contracts
   k. Water meter reading, maintenance and billing - Improve the "meter to cash" cycle. Improve percentage of non-collected customers
   l. Decrease windshield time for service trucks getting supplies, tools or parts for field work

6. Fire Departments:
   a. Consolidation of stations
   b. Reduction in overtime costs
   c. Fire Inspection Process – pre-inspections
   d. Reduction in fires via smoke detector placement and education
   e. Coverage enhancement
   f. Analysis and reduction in EMT/EMS Mine data - causes leverage improvements
   g. Improve Turnout Time - analyze data and reasons for calls
   h. Create an injury prevention program based on a data driven study of firefighter injuries
   i. Reduce False Alarms - mine data and causes to leverage improvements
   j. Scheduling Fire Inspection process and billing opportunities
   k. Fire prevention strategies
   l. 911 call center analysis (including Police)

7. Police Departments:

    a. Report writing - Concentration Diagrams and Check Sheets
    b. Hiring and retention process for dispatchers and standard work for training
    c. Case assignments for investigative services - criteria and process
    d. Jailing Class C misdemeanors
    e. New animal shelter process
    f. Warrant and Court Bailiff functions (consolidate)
    g. Records Division Area - Evidence Rooms - 5S
    h. Review Crime Data - against people and against property, noting trends and focusing on areas to analyze
    i. Consolidate and/or merge layers of reports to be sent to DA
    j. Analyze forms - errors and rework
    k. Private jobs revenue collection and billing process
    l. Police deployment strategies – location and frequency
    m. Improve value added street coverage time
    n. Reduce overtime costs
    o. Accident reporting process improvement
    p. Policies and procedures consolidation
    q. False alarm reductions

8. Parks & Recreation:

    a. Recreation Fund flexibility - create an ability to take advantage of programming opportunities as they arise
    b. Equipment distribution across the city to reduce windshield time
    c. Mowing (internal) - create standard work on how to mow each park, set expected time goals, set quality level
    d. Vehicle organization - standardize vehicle equipment and organization - 5S
    e. Special/Community Event application process
    f. Utilization and maintenance of facilities

9. Human Resources:

    a. Seasonal hiring
    b. Hiring process – from requisition to start date
    c. Timekeeping and payroll - review process
    d. Worker's comp/liability claims/contract review
    e. New hire paperwork in processing/onboarding

10. Health & Human Services:

    a. Grants management of funds – collections, disbursements, contract management, etc.
    b. Title 8 management – "one-stop shopping" for clients and customers
    c. Library analysis and consolidation
    d. Elder care reduction in house fires
    e. Restaurant inspection and fines process
    f. Handling displaced tenants
    g. Blighted properties management and flow
    h. Property auction process

11. Economic Development –

    a. All licensing and inspection processes
    b. Business retention
    c. Business recruitment
    d. Remove unnecessary codes and regulations
    e. Hook up and disconnect issues - causes and data
    f. Cycle times to get businesses up and running.

12. Environmental Services:

    a. Pretreatment and grease trap inspection
    b. Water/Wastewater Laboratory - sample processing
    c. Significant industrial user inspection process
    d. Environmentally sensitive area inspections
    e. Restaurant inspections and oversight
    f. Construction sites - inspections reporting

13. Engineering:

    a. Engineering plans and documents storage and retrieval – 5S
    b. New business development plan approvals

14. Revenue enhancements

    a. Consistent enforcement of all regulations and collections of fines

K-12 Schools:

1. Consolidate duplications with City or County departments
2. HR processes
3. Purchasing processes
4. Finance processes
5. Grants processes
6. Off-hours facility revenues
7. Facilities maintenance
8. Full review of non-classroom costs and wastes
9. Asset tracking with employee transfers

CHAPTER SUMMARY: The above areas are some examples in cities, counties and K-12 school systems where a Lean Government approach has been applied. There are also many examples in State Government agencies where Lean Government techniques have been applied. Lean Government has no apparent process limitations when it comes to improving service, capacity, and employee engagement while reducing wastes and costs.

Chapter 17
Lean Government – NOW! Recap

"It doesn't matter when you start as long as you commence immediately"
Dr. Deming at one of his four day seminars

The economic situation facing Government to provide more services and capacity while at the same time dealing with constant revenue pressures is the impetus to initiate a Lean Government approach. We have covered the reasons why Lean Government initiatives fail toward the end of Chapter 3 on Change Management, so it's not as easy as it looks.

Top Government leadership is pulled in different directions with many competing priorities:
- Too many constituencies with too many goals to be satisfied
- Too many problems are not clearly understood, yet solutions are thrown at them
- Too little knowledge or time to decide what to do
- Too little political will to truly decide what is the best strategic direction to go, over political party and constituency obligations
- Too many services offered to know what are the best to choose
- Too many management teams feel this "Lean Government stuff" is easy and "we've got this" while totally underestimating what it truly takes to be successful and sustainable

Today, the encouraging aspect about Lean Government is there are many initiatives already underway and the learning experience scar tissue already exists:
- There must be a commitment by top leadership to be Lean proficient themselves, be visible, and be actively driving the Lean Government journey
- There are success models which encompass broader Lean Government deployments
- There are training materials available through numerous Government websites.   See: **http://leangovcenter.com/govweb.htm**
- There are hundreds of Kaizen projects that have been done and are accessible through the same websites
- There are key Lean Government principles you need to know that are covered in this book

Lean Government is truly the best way to increase capacity, service, and employee engagement while minimizing costs and wastes.

GET STARTED – NOW!

Index

Made in the USA
Lexington, KY
28 November 2017